TOUCHING *the* CROSS

Real people, real testimonies

Basia Armitage

JEREMY MILLS
PUBLISHING LIMITED

Published by Jeremy Mills Publishing Limited
www.jeremymillspublishing.co.uk

Text © Basia Armitage

First Published 2008

ISBN 978-1-906600-13-6

ACKNOWLEDGEMENTS

First and foremost, I would like to sincerely thank Colin and Sue Cooper of Huddersfield Christian Fellowship for entrusting me with the task of gathering together the inspirational accounts of their congregants' lives. You are a blessing to so many of us. To Sue Cooper and Julie Walker who tirelessly employed their proof-reading skills, I couldn't have done it without you. Jeremy and Hazel at Jeremy Mills Publishing, thank you for your patience and support. To all my friends and family who have encouraged me throughout the process, especially my husband, Peter, who has been behind me every step of the way, I'm so grateful to have you in my life.

And last but certainly not least, a very special thank you goes to all those who had the courage to come forward with the personal accounts of their lives.

Dedicated to the memory of Jerry Lewis, dear friend and brother in Christ. We will never forget you.

CONTENTS

INTRODUCTION

*'... we speak of what we know, and we testify to
what we have seen'* (John 3.11)

Time after time I have sat on the edge of my seat captivated by
the testimonies of people I know and see at church every Sunday,
people who have had an extraordinary and life-changing encounter
with a loving and relational God. People such as Colin who grew up
surrounded by the occult and whose home at the age of seventeen
was a coal shed but who is now the pastor of a thriving and vibrant
church and Jim, saved from a drug-fuelled personal hell.

Taken aback by such abundant and clear evidence of God working
in the lives of people in an old mill town in West Yorkshire,
England and who happen to attend the same church, I approached
the pastor of Huddersfield Christian Fellowship, Colin Cooper
and his wife, Sue, with a proposal for getting these testimonies
into print. They wholeheartedly approved and suggested that I
make an appeal for any other church members who felt they had
a testimony to share. Many did and the result is this book.

Testimonies of transformed lives related to me in the form of
an interview are interspersed with specific events written and
submitted by the congregants themselves. The reported accounts
are as varied and individual as the people themselves. Life stories
run alongside reports of healings, restored relationships and
freedom from bondage to destructive lifestyles.

Upon completing Touching the Cross, I noticed certain patterns
clearly emerging. Of the fifteen people showcased, three had

unmistakably heard God's voice resulting in dramatic and hope-filled, life-altering changes; four, the lifting of deep depressions; and in many cases, prayer was seen to be the precursor of healings. What is also clear is that those who had undergone suffering and through it had experienced a real and loving God, had themselves gone on to become catalysts, perhaps unknowingly, for significant physical and/or psychological breakthroughs in others who are also to be found in the pages of this book.

Let me say at the outset that this manuscript is not meant as an advertisement for Huddersfield Christian Fellowship. It is simply intended to be a witness to the power released when we metaphorically 'touch the Cross' and enter into a personal and transforming relationship with Jesus Christ. It is evidence of a God who is alive and working here and now. Not just sporadically in the select few who fulfil certain criteria and tick all the right 'holy' boxes, but in the harassed person queueing at the supermarket checkout, the rich and successful businessman who appears to have it all or the alcoholic we're so careful to avoid. Read on and see why they can all confidently agree with the words of the apostle Paul when he says '… to him who is able to do immeasurably more than all we ask or imagine, according to his power that is at work within us …' (Ephesians 3:20).

Basia Armitage

JAMES SINGH (JIM)

Christmas is My Time

Whether joyfully caught up in the Sunday morning worship, his compact frame 'pogo-ing' to the thrumming beat, animatedly talking ten to the dozen with friends and strangers alike, or expressing his ardent faith in powerful prayer, Jim Singh's wholehearted enjoyment of life is easily discernible. The term 'exuberant' best describes this dynamic young man. The word, itself derived from the Latin *exuberare*[1] or being abundantly fruitful, does justice to the work of God in his life. As Christians we are exhorted to 'produce fruit in keeping with repentance' (Matthew 3:8), God's presence in our lives outwardly manifesting itself in 'love, joy, peace, patience, kindness, goodness, faithfulness, gentleness and self-control' (Galatians 5:22-23). Jesus tells us that we cannot bear fruit unless we remain in Him (John 15:4) and Jim can testify to this truth: 'I get up there on Sunday morning and it's a celebration,' he professes. Referring to the waving of banners in praise as practised in the church, he says: 'I lift the flag and I celebrate God's victory in my life because it was going nowhere and truly once I was blind, but now I can see.'

Actually at one time Jim's life was headed somewhere, but his destructive internal compass was set firmly on a course pointing directly towards the local mortuary via the twin bearings of casualty or prison ...

---

1   Pearsall J (Ed) (2002) *Concise Oxford English Dictionary* 10th Edition Revised, Oxford University Press

Born Narinder Singh but later adopting an English Christian name, Jim was born to Sikh parents who had emigrated to England in the late 1960s. 'I considered myself a Sikh because that's what I was born into,' he says. 'I wouldn't say I was devout or anything, but certainly I was encouraged to read the Sikh scriptures and that was my first taste of religion.'

As a young child, Jim remembers all was not well in the Singh household. 'I had to grow up really fast,' he states. 'I remember that my dad used to drink, but up until I was about six or seven years old, I don't remember him getting really violent. But things went downhill after he started drinking a lot, and I think that's probably when the trouble actually started, and that's when things got really bad. He used to work in textiles, both my parents did, but slowly over the years he eventually lost his job. He got himself another job, he was always able to get another job, but slowly the drink eventually got him to the point where he couldn't hold down a job and couldn't really work, and he was just drinking all the time. But the worst aspect of the alcohol was the violence against me from an early age or actually beating Mum really badly and that really affected me.' One of Jim's earliest memories is of waking up early at the weekends and racing into his parents' bedroom. Diving on to the bed and snuggling up to his sleeping father, he would lay on top of him until he nodded off, whereupon he would be gently moved aside so that his dad's disturbed slumber could be resumed. 'But the first time I actually saw my dad really throwing his weight around and properly laying into my mum I stopped doing it,' he continues. 'I knew what was in him. I'd seen that side of him.'

Weekends were the worst. 'My dad would get drunk and Mum and Dad would start fighting and he would then start lashing out,'

Jim explains. These episodes became a part of everyday life in the Singh household. Jim remembers as a child rapidly becoming desensitised to the sight of blood following a fight and recalls chilling episodes of wiping blood out of blown vinyl wallpaper: 'It had dried and I had to get my nail into it to get it all out. And I'd get the liquid detergent out and it was fantastic for cleaning the blood out of the wallpaper. I'd clean and tidy the house of all the things that had been broken.'

These recollections are clearly painful for Jim. 'It's difficult but one of the things about the Lord is that when you meet Him, all these memories fade away,' he says. I suppose you never forget because you can sit and really think about it and you can remember those times again. But they're hard to come to mind and it's just a testimony to what God has done. He just heals it.'

Several incidents, however, highlight the violence and terror that characterised Jim's and his siblings' early life. 'I remember seeing my sister,' he says. 'She was trying to protect my mum by dragging Dad off her and she got hit on the head with a screwdriver. I remember there was blood everywhere, my mum was being thrown around, I'd taken a bit of a beating and I remember I was barefoot. I think I was about eight years old and I ran and ran and ran. I came to a police station not far from my house and told them what was happening. They came round and we began to realise that perhaps there was some help out there; the police could do something about these things. There were many times that the police came over for a disturbance but my dad would never change. He used to be in jail, used to be on probation, went to Alcoholics Anonymous, he even ended up in a mental institution for drying out. And in all this time my mum was still religious and I used to ask: "Mum, why does this kind of thing happen? Why does it happen to us? Where's God? Why doesn't God stop it?" Mum would talk to me about prayer but it was more a reading of the Sikh scriptures and I suppose that was a bit like praying.

'But I remember one particular occasion,' Jim pronounces, his expressive brown eyes bright with unshed tears. 'I remember it as the moment I gave up on any notion of there being a God. Even if I think about it now, it still chokes me up. Not so much that I remember the pain of what happened, but the fact that it was the moment when I said: 'From this day on, I will never have anything to do with a God and I will look for answers elsewhere.' What happened was that my dad, in a fit of rage, had attacked my mum and she was just covered in blood. We managed to get her upstairs into the bedroom. We'd got clever by this time – my dad would use implements and as soon as he got like this we used to go and get the knives, hide the knife tray, go and get the screwdriver and get all the tools (because he used to try and use tools to get through the door behind which we were hiding). On this occasion we had actually unscrewed the outer and inner door handle but left the door closed. I had taken the pin out so there was no latch to open the door with and he didn't know how the latch worked. We knew that the only way for him to get in was to break it down. We heard him going outside to the garage and we were in the bedroom, all of us - my mum on the bed nursing her wounds and me and my three sisters holding the door. We didn't know what was going to happen. I positioned myself against the door (at the time I was small enough to actually stand upright with my shoulder against the door handle) and all of a sudden we heard this BANG! BANG! BANG! And he just went hell for leather. He was absolutely hammering this door down and the door frame was shattering. I remember the plaster coming off the walls. We knew that once he got in there, he had hammers, he had everything. He was going to come in there like a blaze of fire and we really thought that that was the night. That was it. We were going to die that night. My mum was screaming and that was one of my worst memories, hearing my mum scream. And if you have ever heard a woman being properly beaten and in total despair … there was just this howl, what I could only describe as howling, and it was awful. There was us guys trying to hold the door closed and the door frame and the lock shattered. Eventually it got to about two in the morning and the door was beginning to bend in the middle because he had taken that much wood from the outside skin of the door. And the carpet was ruffling back. Every time my dad would try and get in a little bit, the door would open and our feet would slide and the carpet ruffled and we'd shut the door again. And every time he'd try and get his fingers round the door, we'd whack them with a hammer.

'My sister said: 'Run outside and see if there's somebody there,' because we couldn't phone anybody, the phone was downstairs. And so I ran to the window and saw someone coming. I opened the casement window and lifted myself up so I could get my head over it, I was only a little kid, and I shouted out to this guy. I said: "Please, please, will you just phone the police. My dad's gonna kill us. You can hear him banging, he's got hammers and everything. Will you please phone the police?" He just paused, I'll never forget it, he paused and looked up and then he looked down towards his feet and he said: "No, I won't' and he just carried on walking. And this guy, he was the only hope, there was no-one else up and down the street, nothing, not even a car. And he just carried on walking, carried on walking. And I just shouted out to him: 'PLEASE!" and he could hear the screams of my sisters and my mum inside the house but he carried on walking.

'My mum cottoned on to what had happened. As I stood there I heard her saying: "Don't worry, he's not going to hurt you. I won't let him. Come and sit on the bed with me." And as a kid, that's what you want to hear; but as I turned towards her, I looked her in the eye and I was only a little kid but I *knew* she didn't believe it at all. I could just tell. So as my sisters huddled up round her I just ran towards the door and slammed my body up against it, pressing with all my might. The banging, which had temporarily stopped, started up again and I realised that he was now using an axe. The door was really bending and bowing in the middle now and I was literally bouncing off it. Finally, the blade of the axe came through and there was plaster all over my head but I still kept pushing against the door, because I knew if he got in, that was it.

'All of a sudden, he stopped. He pulled the axe out of the door and it fell with a thud. Then he walked into the next room and just collapsed on to the bed. And that was it. That was the end of the night. He'd absolutely zonked himself out. But that day I said: "No! What I saw today, the whole thing of what happened today, there can't be a God. There can't be a God. I don't want to know a God who will allow this kind of thing to happen." I literally spoke out those words and I said: "From this day I will never, ever recognise You as being there ever again." I was a kid at junior school at the time, and I said that.'

Possessed of an enquiring, analytical mind, Jim discovered science and it opened up a whole new world: 'I was mad about science, I loved it. My friends used to call me Boff (short for Boffin) because

I used to know everything, you know. I could tell you how far the nearest star was … I was just full of general knowledge. Suddenly the answers that I wanted seemed to be found in science and, OK, so it didn't have all the answers such as who started off the Big Bang but for me it was just a matter of time before science told me where all this came from.'

The accumulation of events at home, though, spiralled out of control along an ever more destructive trajectory and Jim's tortured childhood developed into a troubled and wretched adolescence. His sister ran away from home and the Social Services, alerted, placed her in a safe house. Jim, although at times moving in with his friends, stayed with his parents. 'I would stand up to my father and end up getting a beating,' he says. 'One particular day he came at me with a hammer and I remember this hammer brushing past my head and slamming into the kitchen sink. I just ran. I got hold of this hammer and I ran. I got all my friends together and told them what had happened and they said that that was it. They were going to sort my dad out. And that day we absolutely leathered him: metal bars, blocks of wood – five of us including one guy who was older than us at twenty-seven. We were only about fourteen-years-old. I remember we had him up against the garden wall and I rested the hammer against his head so he could feel the cold. I was speaking to him in Punjabi and my friends thought I was scaring him, saying: "You mess with me again, I'm gonna kill you". But really I was saying: "Time to say goodbye Dad. This is where it ends," because by this time I had become sick and twisted. I remember I used to wake up in a cold sweat, wanting to smash his head in. I loved the film where an obsessed fan inflicted pain on a bed-ridden author, because that's where I got my inspiration from. I wanted to tie him to a bed where no-one knew and just torture him, literally torture him. I used to sleep with knives in my bed, because in a way I wanted him to attack me just so I could stab him. So by the time of this incident, I was all fired up and ready: "This is where it ends," I said and lifted up the hammer. Fortunately, I was being closely watched by one of my friends and in a fraction of a second, he realised what I was about to do. As I started to swing the hammer down he yelled: "NO!" and shielded my dad. I nearly broke his arm – he had put his arm in the way and then they all tried to grab me before the hammer came down on my dad's head.

'And that day, even my friends were shocked, because we were like young yobbos. They were going to give my dad a good duffing up but no-one intended murder. So when they realised what I had almost done, they told me I was nuts. But from that day, my father *never* beat my mum, because I told him: "You will never do this again. The day you even touch my sisters or my mum again, that will be the end."

'Then started years of just me and him. Just absolute hatred. I used to sleep with a piece of wood because he used to come in and try to beat me and it just got worse.

'I also began to get involved in crime. At the time I considered myself smart intellectually and I became very adept at obtaining monies by deception: forgery, stealing from establishments, and that is what I became good at. I used to plan operations months in advance and soon had fraudulently acquired thousands of pounds. I moved away from home and was subjected to the world outside: clubbing, drinking, drugs. Suddenly *I* was in control. I could do what I wanted, I could have anything I wanted, and it was OK to have it.

'But it was a mess. My life was a mess. I couldn't go anywhere without getting mugged because it had become known that I had money. I paid someone to steal a car for me. I had no driving licence, no insurance, nothing. I was fifteen and I was driving around in a Golf GTi. One day I was high on LSD and I said to myself: "Right. It's time to end it now. It's time to go back home, I need to finish it with my dad." So I planned it all, I can remember writing it all out: "He'll attack me. He'll hit me like this. I'll get a few cuts and bruises, let him give me a good going over. Everybody knows that something's building up between me and my dad. It would be self-defence and I'd pretty much get away with it because the history is there." This is what I thought. And I planned it all out and I was literally going to murder my dad. I was going to allow him to hit me, which I knew he would, and then I was going to stab him in the neck with a knife, or hit him with a hammer.'

Jim went downstairs and phoned his parents' house. His father answered. Yes, he was drunk all right. He clicked the receiver back on its cradle. Right. He was going to make it happen now. He was going to face his father and kill him. At that moment, the doorbell rang. One of his close friends stood on the doorstep. He had recently succeeded in getting through to the regional finals of the Young Inventor of the Year competition and was calling to take Jim up on his offer of supporting him at the contest, which happened to be taking place that very day. Intent on carrying out his mission, Jim initially refused to go with him. His friend pleaded. He didn't want to go on his own and be intimidated by the crowds. Jim found himself relenting. His friends meant a lot to him, they'd seen him through many bad times; he finally agreed to go along. His determination to end the life of his father that day though, still held firm. It would just have to be postponed until he returned. 'I was resolute,' he asserts. 'It was going to happen. He was going to die.

'And my friend won the regional finals,' he smiles. 'Great day. Great day out. Came back to his house late in the afternoon and while I'm there his phone rings. It's my sister for me: "I think you'd better come home. Dad's dead." She told me that she and Mum had come home and found him at the bottom of the steps. I couldn't believe it. On the day when I had intended murder, he was found dead. And literally everybody thought that I had killed him. It wasn't until the Coroner's Report came out that it was established that he'd drunk himself to death. The local newspaper headlined it as *The Highest Blood-Alcohol Level the Coroner Has Ever Seen*. And I would have killed him that day – I really would have killed him.

'We cremated him and I was as cold as ice. I remember being there at the funeral, showing absolutely no emotion. I didn't shed a single tear until I met the Lord, regarding the fact that my dad had died.'

At the time, Jim just felt elated. Here was freedom at last! Moving back into the family home with his mother and sisters, he was king of his castle. No more restraints! Life was sweet. However, his new found liberation resulted in dropping out of college, where he had been pursuing qualifications in chemistry, biology and psychology, and getting more involved in criminal activities, organising several successful bank raids.

'As a person, I was a popular guy,' he says. 'But I was a nasty piece of work. I was nasty, nasty, nasty. I used to think I'd never be like my dad, but I remember flying off the handle, just like him and absolutely going ballistic. I'd have my little mum, who I'd done so much to protect, up against the wall by her throat. I used to beat my sisters with blocks of wood, anything as an excuse to slam their head against a table. I thought nothing of it. And inside there was this pent-up rage. I felt almost as if my dad had got the easy way out. I was absolutely gutted and angry that he'd got such an easy way out. I had had plans for him. I used to love waking with a shiver, in a cold sweat, because I'd been dreaming about what I wanted to do with him – all the horrible ways I could really torture him. That's what I was like. That's the kind of person I'd become. Clever, stealing, living a lifestyle way beyond my means, attacking my family. A nasty person.

'I used to go clubbing with my friends, drugged up, taking Ecstasy, speed, amphetamines. We'd be out all night: Liverpool, Birmingham, Leeds, everywhere, getting back into Huddersfield on Sunday morning at nine o'clock. Then I started work, I got a job making plug sockets, and I got horrendous depression. I used to sit in my room looking out of the window and just cry.

'At that time, my best friend became a Christian and he used to try to talk to me about God all the time. All the time. He knew what I was like. When it came to things of God I used to try and convince girls to have abortions: "Oh, just have an abortion," I thought nothing of it, I was completely emotionless. "It's going to ruin your life." I used to try and convince them with all my heart that there was nothing after life. And I remember this Christian at school and I used to just rip her apart, I used to bully her until there were tears in her eyes, just because she had something to say about a God. That's how against it all I was. But yet this one person was my friend. He was the one person who I couldn't do that with, I couldn't just drop that friendship. We'd known each other that long it was beyond falling out.

'He started bringing me to Huddersfield Christian Fellowship and the only way he could get me in there was when I was on drugs; he had given up drugs at this point. This was the church we used to walk past, laughing, when we came out of the train station at nine o'clock in the morning. While I was high on Ecstasy, he used to say to me: "You love me, don't you? We're like brothers. Just come to church with me today," and I used to go with him. Salt all round my face from dancing all night, bottle of water in my hand, shaking because I'd got the shakes from the drugs and I'd sit at the back of the Fellowship Centre laughing, just laughing. What a bunch of idiots, I thought. They all think they're worshipping God and they're just going to get to the end and die, it's just so sad.

'And this is where I was. A nasty, horrible person, now wracked by depression, on drugs, stealing, and my life was going downhill and heading fast, at lightning speed, towards something. Either jail, because I was getting more and more confident in the things I was doing, stealing bigger and bigger amounts of money; or hospital, as I was getting in deeper with drugs, stepping it up all the time, staying out all hours, vicious when angry. I had become what my dad had been, and more.

'But every now and then I'd go to church. I was there one Sunday in December 1996. It was the morning service before the evening Christmas Celebration. I'd got to know a few people there so it wasn't as scary going in. I didn't feel as isolated. I remember sitting there and listening to a guest preacher, a close friend of

Colin who is the pastor of Huddersfield Christian Fellowship. I can't remember what the sermon was about, but at the end there was an appeal: "While everyone's head is bowed and their eyes are closed, who wants to give their lives to Jesus Christ?" I thought I felt what in those days I could only describe as a warm feeling inside, but I just crushed it and pushed it out of the way. My friends gave me a nudge: "Just give your life now, don't be stupid." But I wouldn't.

'I left the service that morning and went to my favourite secluded spot, the local cemetery. For some reason I used to like going there. I knew I was alone, I could go and sit on a bench and be surrounded by loads of dead people. There was just something about it, I don't know what. As I was sitting there, though, I started asking some questions: "God, if You're there, why did these things happen to me and my family?" I went through the usual "why do bad things happen to good people?" All the reasons and questions that any analytical mind comes up with. "How can there be a God? How can You be there when all this has happened? In fact, if You are there, I don't want to know You".'

Despondent and alone, Jim returned home and switched on the television. The first channel featured a Christmas service for young people who were being encouraged to get rid of all the psychological baggage and pain in their lives by symbolically dropping it all in a dustbin. 'And I just stood there,' Jim looks back. 'And tears welled up in my eyes as these kids, teenagers, were going up to this bin and placing their closed fists over it and then opening their hands as if to drop what the world has put on them into the bin. The bin was at the foot of the Cross, and I didn't understand what the Cross was. I didn't understand that there was power in the Cross. I turned to a different channel, it was *Songs of Praise*. I turned to another channel and it was something else about Jesus. It just seemed as if somebody was trying to get my attention. I had tried all day to get away from these thoughts of giving your life, this voice and this warm feeling of urgency in my heart. In the end I literally became so fatigued I just couldn't take it any more.' His voice cracking with emotion, Jim explains what happened next. 'I asked: "What happened when I cried out to that guy on the street? Where were You?" And at that moment I knew God was listening to me. I could feel it. A peace that I can't explain came upon me as I realised that He does exist. Suddenly I remembered the gospel message at church that morning, and in my mind the pressing needs for answers as to why all the bad things had happened to me were in a flash superseded by my realisation that *I* was in need of forgiveness for *my own sins*. I realised that I had no option but to make my peace with God.

'So I went back to the Fellowship Centre for the evening Christmas Celebration service. I went and sat on my own, without any of my friends and it was the same preacher from the morning service. That evening he talked about giving presents at Christmas and that God had given us a gift, His own Son, Jesus Christ, but there's nothing really that we can give Him in return. The only thing we can offer Him is our lives. As soon as he said that and asked if anybody wanted to give their lives to Him, my hand shot up. I was the first person to put their hand up, and he saw it, but I don't remember anything else he might have said after that point because something just washed over me and I felt a warmth which I now know was God's Holy Spirit. And God just moved into my life. Into this hard, evil, depressed, angry person there came this intense love. *Intense*. It was absolutely wonderful and I just burst into tears, and I'm talking I couldn't close my eyes for the tears that were just rolling out of my eyes. And I just cried, and I cried, and I cried and I cried.'

Tears often accompany, and are an indication of, God's presence when He is allowed access into lives. David Wilkerson, the country preacher who made it his mission to reach out to violent gang members in New York, sees it like this:

'I think I could almost put it down as a rule that the touch of God is marked by tears. When finally we let the Holy Spirit into our innermost sanctuary, the reaction is to cry. I have seen it happen again and again. Deep soul-shaking tears, weeping rather than crying. It comes when that last barrier is down and you surrender yourself to health and to wholeness. And when it does come, it ushers forth such a new personality that, from the days of Christ on, the experience has been spoken of as a birth. "You must be born again," said Jesus. And the paradox is this: at the heart of this newborn personality is joy; yet the joy is ushered in by tears.'[2]

Jim was going through the process of dying to his old self and being born again into his newly-awakened spiritual life in Christ. Amazingly, along with the tears, in the same way that many people close to death see their lives flashing before their eyes, he experienced the same phenomenon.

'I'll never forget it,' he says. 'It was like a newsreel, it was like you see on TV. It was like a flashing by, an explanation of the deep,

---

2   Wilkerson, David; with Sherrill, Elizabeth and Sherrill, John (2002 Edition) *The Cross and the Switchblade*, Zondervan p 84

crushing questions I needed to have answered. Literally at that moment, at what to me when I was crying felt like an hour, God took me back to the scene where I cried out to that guy in the street. And He said, and I remember His voice, He said: "I never left you. I didn't leave you for one moment. I knew exactly what was happening. I was in control and I let it happen because I knew you were stronger than that. I knew you could handle it. I knew you were going to be able to take it. I was going to turn it for good. I'm going to turn you into something … I'm going to bring out good from something that was going to be so bad. And the person you've turned into, I'm going to turn into something more." I was just crying as He said this, and He said: "Let me show you that I never left you. It's the way you see things and the way that your eyes have been blinded to my presence in your life. I never left you. When you cried out to that person, I let you go to that very point where you were so broken inside that you knew you were absolutely helpless and so you cried out to one person on the street that you thought could help you. But I let that person say no because while you had no hope, in my heart there was hope that you might turn to me and say – "God, get me out of this" – but you didn't. But deep in your heart something was happening. I didn't let that person help you or save you, because I wanted on *this* day to show that I was there. I helped you. You ran to that door and you held that door closed. It took four of you to hold that door closed and you barely did it then. You were only eight at the time. Do you really think it was you that held that door closed?" And I just cried all the more because it was so true. How *did* I manage to do it on my own? And then God said: "I held that door closed because I said – 'This far you can come, and no further' – and that's where the night ended because I pushed you to that point to show you now that it was me, not you." And of course He was right, it wasn't me. All these years I'd been blind to the times when God had been there for me, and that was just one of them. By simply saying: "It was me that held the door closed," I knew. He was there on the day I was going to kill my dad. I'm telling you, I was absolutely resolute. And it just so happened that my friend won the finals and on that day he had to go to the regionals and he came to get me to go with him. It was almost like God took that away from me at that point. And if He hadn't done, where would I have been? In jail? Gone crazy because I'd murdered someone? What would I have been like?

'The scenes stopped. I stood up and a church member came over and led me to the privacy of a quiet room to pray. I didn't know what to do, I'd never prayed before but I was led through the Sinner's Prayer asking forgiveness for my sins and thanking Jesus for dying on the Cross for me. I cried and cried as I prayed this prayer. Literally from that point I felt all the baggage, everything I was carrying, just fall off me. I came to the Cross and it just fell off me and the depression lifted. Never again did I sit in a room and just cry and feel like that again; a joy came into my life. I'm not saying that everything was suddenly all right, but my old self was dying, and not slowly either. It was like it was just being cut off me with a chainsaw!

'My mum, when I came home, couldn't believe the person that I was – couldn't believe I'd turned to God. She wasn't bothered whether I was a Sikh or not, she was just so glad that I believed in God. People who had known me for years used to walk up to me on the street weeks and months afterwards and ask what had happened to me. I hadn't said anything to them but just from my countenance, from the look on my face, they knew I was different.

And I was, I'd met with Jesus and my life was totally transformed. From then on there was an unravelling of my entire life and God began to work on things in my heart. The way I was as a person, my character, everything. The drugs stopped for a start, as did the swearing. But something that took a while to go was the anger, because even though I could control it, it was still there just waiting for the right trigger. And I remember one day as a Christian, I lunged for my mum. We were having a big fight and I grabbed her by the throat and I thought: "God, what am I doing here?" And I said: "God, I want this gone. I want it gone and I can't do it alone." I remember crying and thinking that I couldn't stop it. I'd tried hard but it was still there, so I said to God: "Lord, I want this anger, this rage to go. I can't stop it, I realise that now and if You don't do it, no-one is going to." The next time my mum started badgering and nagging me, because she used to do that, just when she'd pushed me to that point where previously I'd have flipped, I felt it all just wash over me, like water off a duck's back. From then on I was able to walk away from explosive confrontations and I never experienced that rage again. Never. And that was the Lord. That is one of the greatest things the Lord ever did for me.'

Three months later Jim was baptised as an outward sign of his inner commitment. He couldn't have been happier; he really meant business now. But within two weeks he was being arrested for a bank raid he had committed two years previously.

'I couldn't believe it,' he declares. 'Here I was, now a Christian. My whole life perspective had changed. I'd gone from working in a plug factory to a day release job at a textile company and things weren't on the up but at least I'd got myself a proper job. I was nineteen-years-old and I was going to be sent down to prison.

I knew that as a Christian I couldn't lie and wangle my way out of it. I didn't know what to do, so I went to see Colin, my pastor: "Colin, why has this happened? I thought I was forgiven!" And I remember the first lesson he taught me was that forgiveness is one thing, but the consequence of sin is quite another. "God has forgiven you," he told me, "but now you're living out the consequence of what you've done."

'I was in turmoil. I didn't want to lose my job and I didn't want to get sent down. So I prayed and asked God to help me; then I went to the police and admitted everything. They couldn't believe it, I'm sure they didn't expect me to confess like that. I can't be sure but I felt that they'd had all this evidence against me for a long time but were confident I'd do the same thing again and then they'd have double ammunition to be able to take me down for something big. I told them all about the way I used to be and how my life had changed since meeting Jesus Christ. As I was leaving the interview, one of the police officers just put his hand on my shoulder and said: "You know, James, I believe you've changed, mate. You might want to give this particular solicitor a ring to help you." Even the police were helping me by giving me the name of a good solicitor who had the right standing with the magistrates and wasn't known as a guy who tries to get every Tom, Dick and Harry off. He was fair, he'd give you a fair shot. So I went to see him and I don't think he wanted to hear that I'd done it. But I told him anyway.

'Then, before I went to court, I had to tell my bosses what was going on and that I might get sent down. I'd been there a few months and they'd seen me before, and they'd seen me after I became a Christian. And I remember saying: "Lord, whatever happens now, I really don't want to lose my job." So I went in and told one of the directors there at the time. He was absolutely flabbergasted and he said: "But you know something, Jim, I know you've changed. I absolutely know you've changed. We'll stand up and testify that you've changed. You're not that person. I know there's something, I don't know what it is but I know there's something. You can use our solicitors if you want. Don't worry about your job; I don't think you'll get sent down but if you do, your job is still here as soon as you come back out." I was so amazed! He then asked if there was anything else I was worried about and I told him I didn't know how I'd pay off the amount I'd stolen. I said: "I'll be forced to pay it back but I want to pay it back as well," and he said, "Well, we'll pay half." I'd been in that company a lot less than a year and yet such was the transformation in my life, I believe, that this guy just saw something in me and said: "I don't want this guy to struggle. I want this guy to be working here in my company." He said, "We'll pay half." And I couldn't believe it. It was like God was taking that from me as well.

'And I remember going to the court and standing in front of the magistrates. The bank hadn't even put in a claim for compensation so theoretically I didn't have to pay it back. Anyway the magistrates went out for deliberation and I was sent out of the room until they came back in. As I stood outside I said: "Lord, whatever happens in here, You've done so much. You died for me on the Cross, you saved me. I asked you that I wouldn't lose my job, I've got hope in this job and I want to make a go of it. I'm not taking that half. I'm not going to take a penny of their money, I'm going to pay it all back." And I went in and the magistrate said words to the effect of: "Based on the police report and your admission, we believe you've changed. Because of that we're not imposing any court costs of this trial, but regarding the compensation to the bank, unfortunately it's a large amount of money and it has to be paid back. However as magistrates, we have taken the decision to order you to pay back half of what you stole." Half of what I stole! And I'd just testified five minutes before that that I wouldn't take money from my company. It was as if God had said: "Well OK, I'll halve it anyway." And I couldn't believe it! My eyes welled up. I was going to pay this money back, but to have it halved! I just couldn't believe it.

'I just thanked the Lord and went back to my company. My director was still insistent that his previous offer still stood but I refused: "No. You've done enough. I'll pay this back." Now I didn't know what the repercussions of that would be, but after that I just had so much favour at work. Whatever I put my hand to, whatever task I was given at work, God blessed and helped me prosper. I progressed in the company and succeeded in many areas, being given different roles over the years.

'So I had this story, I had this testimony to tell people that I had come from nothingness to this day release course and progression in a textile company. And schools wanted to hear about it. I used to go along and organise workshops and motivate the pupils. I'd tell them that the fact that they couldn't get a degree wasn't an issue. It was all in the mind; there was a lot more out there for them and there were other ways to get into university. I was advocating a training scheme at the time and that came to the attention of a well-known company within the photographic industry. They asked me to be a speaker at the launch of their training programme and I stood up in front of 250 people, among them the heads of two leading photographic companies, and told them of the success that I'd had. They were just so amazed and came to encourage me afterwards.

'After that, the Government asked me to attend the European Presidency and I gave a speech to the European Ministers which was translated into fifteen languages. As I was speaking it was simultaneously being translated to all these people and it was being projected on to a board and it was just fantastic! Then one day, not long afterwards, I opened an envelope at home which had the Royal Crest on it. It was an invite and I've still got it. It said: *The Master of the household has received Her Majesty's command to invite Mr James Singh to a reception to be held at Buckingham Palace on June 1st 1998.* I was going to meet the Queen! She was holding a reception for young achievers who had excelled in their particular field. And just little old me from Huddersfield ... I was going to meet the Queen! It was in all the local papers. My life had changed so much. I had a joy in my heart because I had the Lord in my life and I could see Him working. I could see Him turning not just little cogs, but big cogs.

'God is really working in my life now and providing for me, even my house. I started looking for a house a few years ago because I thought it was time to move out of home, but I couldn't afford the asking prices. Then my director at work told me he was selling his house: 'I'm having a new house built, Jim, and I know you're looking to buy and I thought – 'Why don't I just sell it to Jim?' – Because I know if he says he's going to buy it, he's going to buy it. He's a man of his word and he won't let me down in the middle of the sale so that my house falls through as well." Then he said: "I'll give you the house at a good price and I'll pass on the cost that I would have paid to an estate agent to you." He sold me this house in the boom of the housing market at a price where it would have just disappeared off the market in seconds. And then because I didn't have the deposit to get a mortgage he said: "Don't worry.

I'll lend you the deposit." So he lent me the deposit and he gave me the house at such a low price that the mortgage I could afford, I could get anyway and pay off the deposit. So I suddenly ended up with a house and a mortgage without a deposit that I had to pay! But that's not all. While we were doing the deal, as time was going on and his house was being built and I was getting ready to move in, he said to me: "Jim, I'm buying all new stuff for my house so I'm leaving everything in the house as long as you can give me a hand making up all the furniture in my new house. I'm no good at flat-pack furniture." So of course I helped him and he was as good as his word. When he said he was leaving everything, he really meant everything: carpets, curtains, kettle, toaster, washing machine, fridge, pots, pans, cutlery, the lot. Even the fish tank with the fish still in it! So he sold me the house at way below market value, lent me the deposit interest free which I paid back at the end of the month, and on top of that, it was fully and completely furnished. I felt so blessed and I learned the truth of Jesus's words: "A good measure, pressed down, shaken together and running over, will be poured into your lap." (Luke 6:38).

'And I remember on Christmas Eve, almost four years ago, I came with a couple of bags which was all my clothes and my computer and that was it. I'd moved in! Christmas is my time. I became a Christian the Christmas of 1996, so that's eleven years of walking with the Lord and I will always remember the day I stood up as a Christian and sang, 'Hark the herald angels sing! Glory to the new born King', because I was in tears, you know. And honestly, I'll never forget the day of my salvation, never. I can honestly say, eight times out of ten when I'm worshipping the Lord, I remember the day I got saved. If I focus on it and just close my eyes I'm in that place at the Christmas Celebration when I gave my life and I can sense the presence of God. I can smell the atmosphere and I even remember who was sitting there. I will never forget that day and I just loving singing songs about the power of the Cross and how Jesus died for us. I just love it.'

Now I'm Listening

I had always known someone was trying to communicate with me. When my mind was still, which was not very often, there was a niggling feeling that I was not listening; when walking around the garden, a sense that there was someone at my elbow anxious to make His presence felt. But life was good: I had a hard-working successful husband, two healthy, happy daughters; ample money and to spare, a beautiful home and plenty to keep me occupied. I even went to church, although my family decreased the average age of the small traditional established parish congregation by about a half! So what was it that I needed to hear? To whom was I to listen? I remained perplexed because this feeling of someone trying to attract my attention never really left me.

In the autumn of 1989 my daughters were aged eight and five, both at school, and Keith was working long hours as marketing director of a national company based locally. I decided that now was the time to retrain and add to my skills in the hope that I could return to work. So I enrolled at the local college to take a secretarial course. I was out of the house more and I became even busier as I had to balance the course with my domestic and family duties. But I loved the course and the social atmosphere that went with it. The other girls were from different backgrounds but mainly at the same stage in life as I was and this was my opportunity to spread my wings and meet people I would not normally come into contact with. Life was getting even better, or so I thought.

Then in late October I got the first clue that things were not quite right in my marriage. How could this be? I fulfilled my wifely duties: preparing meals, shopping, cleaning the house, doing the laundry, ensuring the children were in the right place at the right time and I was preparing to go out to earn money. But this was not enough. From Keith's point of view, there was something very important missing: warmth, fun, spontaneity and companionship. We began to have terrible rows and restless nights and I started suffering from a pain in my chest, panic, fear, anger and dark despair. Within two months, Keith had left the marital home and moved into a rented flat about fifteen minutes' drive away. Telling the children that Daddy was no longer going to live with us was heartbreaking for everyone. My world was turned upside down. Life can be like that sometimes: one minute you are on top of the world, the next at the bottom. Somehow I kept the secretarial course going: those other girls were my lifeline, my comfort and my encouragement. It was amazing how many of them had gone, or were going through, something similar.

All through this period I continued to attend church and the vicar was a source of practical, emotional and spiritual support. I also continued to read the Bible daily, using Scripture Union reading notes. None of that really changed. What did change was my prayer life. This suddenly became real, desperate, and urgent. From the heart. Now I was listening, now I was needy, now God became real. And now God answered. Suddenly, after all these years, I was in communication with a real and living God.

The turning point came one evening, shortly after Keith had left our home. My mother had travelled up from Kent, a mercy dash to support the children and me in a time of crisis. She was downstairs and I was alone in my bedroom. I was kneeling on the floor against the bed, crying with pain and desolation. I started to pray out loud: 'Jesus, I know You are real, I know You are out there. I have tried everything I know but I cannot cope any more. I have done it my way and it did not work. It's Your turn now. You sort it out for me because I can't.' A simple, heartfelt cry, short but real. I got up from my knees. Nothing tangible happened but I felt a peace come into my heart, a strength, a hope. As I walked slowly downstairs, my mother looked at me. She later said I was a different person from the one who had gone upstairs just twenty minutes earlier.

The circumstances of my life did not change overnight. Keith did not move back home; the days, and especially the nights, did not become easier. The difference was that now I knew I was not alone; there was someone walking through all this darkness with me, alongside me. And not just anyone, but the God of the universe, the God who had created Heaven and the earth, who rules on the throne of all creation, the God who is also my Father in Heaven, the God who is my friend. He loves me, He is committed to me and He wants the very best for me. I knew my Bible. I knew that He had sent His only son, Jesus, to die for me on the cross of crucifixion. Whenever I sinned, that sacrifice was the punishment that should have come to me. Jesus took it in my place. This proves that God loves me. And not only did Jesus do that for me 2,000 years ago, but death could not hold Him. He rose from the dead and He is alive now, living in my heart, helping me each day, talking to me. Jesus was the difference.

Now that I had given control of my life to Jesus, He started to change my character, lead me to other Christians and reorder my priorities. The Bible came alive to me as Jesus made the words jump out from the page. Suddenly stories that had been written thousands of years before applied to a housewife in her thirties living in the Midlands in the late twentieth century. I loved to read the 'love' chapter, 1 Corinthians 13. This described God's love for me and also how I should love Keith. I had got it wrong obviously but now I wanted to get it right, not just in case I was given a second chance in my marriage but also to please Jesus. One verse in particular jumped out at me: 'Love never fails' (verse 8). I used to go to sleep with the Bible on my bed – a sort of 'comfort blanket'. I continued, too, to use Scripture Union's notes but began now to personalise the passages and to apply them to my life and circumstances. I was hungry to hear what God was saying to me and desperate for Him to change my character because I knew this was the best way to live my life. Before, I had lived it my way and I could see the mess I had got into. Now I had a second chance, and I was determined I was not going to waste it.

After about four months, I began to think I needed to meet more Christians and there was one family that kept coming to mind. God was leading me to the mother of one of my elder daughter's school friends. I had met her and her husband occasionally and knew the family was Christian. I had been struck right at the beginning by a difference in the way they lived their lives that I found attractive. However, I had not formed a relationship with this family in my own right and did not meet them regularly. Eventually I plucked up the courage and one day (out of the blue from this lady's point of view) rang her and asked if I could talk to her. She was eager to welcome me and to help. I think I had gone as far as I could on my own and now Jesus wanted me to meet mature Christians who could help me grow. As I talked to her, she realised that she needed to introduce me to another Christian lady. Gradually Jesus was leading me to a group of Christians who could help me grow and mature more than in the church I was attending. At this time, these new friends were in the process of leaving the established church themselves and setting up their own church. In time, I left the traditional church near my home and became a founder member of that newly-formed Christian Fellowship.

Even though I was a young Christian, I knew what I was looking for and needed from a church: dynamic worship, Bible-based teaching and fellowship that would include a single mother and her two children. Over the next three to four years, this new church gave me all that and much more. The members became my extended family, more than just friends, giving me practical support, emotional comfort, spiritual encouragement and guidance. I, in turn, played my part fully, attending all the meetings, producing a weekly newsletter and serving and encouraging others as I could, particularly in the setting up of a prayer strategy for this young church. God was using me to help extend His influence in the locality. But He also had work to do *in me*.

First, there was the need to forgive. So often when I was reading the Bible or Christian books, or listening to sermons in church, the importance of forgiveness was stressed. In Matthew 6, verses 14 to 15, God is quite clear: 'For if you forgive men when they sin against you, your heavenly Father will also forgive you. But if you do not forgive men their sins, your Father will not forgive your sins.' That was so hard. After all, Keith had left *me*. I was the one sinned against, but then I was not innocent and sometimes was all too aware of my own sins. I knew my need of forgiveness from the Father but there was a condition attached – I had to forgive Keith in order to receive forgiveness myself. I was reading Christian books in addition to the Bible where this subject was discussed and where practical pointers were given on how to accomplish this. In the end, I decided to forgive Keith. This was an act of the will, not based upon how I felt. What I had not realised was that this was just the beginning. I could not just forgive him once, but because we were still in contact there were many occasions when I had to forgive, again and again and again. Gradually the process of forgiveness became easier. It did not stop me from being hurt, but I was able to release the pain faster.

Then God taught me how to deal with anger and rejection. One important lesson I had to learn was that it was all right to feel angry but it was not all right to act in anger out of a desire to hurt or for revenge. This response never helped me and I never felt better if I gave into the anger. Again, forgiveness was the right way. Through my reading of Christian books and by listening to sermons, I began to realise that only one person had rejected me – Keith – and this did not make me a bad, unworthy or useless person. There were other important lessons for me to learn: live one day at a time and do not think too far ahead; praise God even when I don't feel like it; be thankful for the little things, there are always people worse off than me. I threw myself into this learning curve. After all, it felt as if I had lost everything, so what else did I have to lose? I grew very quickly.

Just a few months into all this, I was lying in bed one evening, praying and praising God. Suddenly it seemed as if Jesus said to me: 'Sue, shut up.' I stopped in amazement and immediately I was overwhelmed by the love of Jesus. It felt as if somebody was pouring warm water over me and I lay in bed, soaking up this love into every fibre of my being. I drifted off to sleep, convinced that I was going to wake up in Heaven. I felt so close to Jesus. To me that was confirmation that He was real, that He loved me, that He would never leave me. He became my security, my rock, my anchor, an ever-present help in time of trouble. Never would He let me down and still, all these years later, He never has.

I began to attend church conferences. This was the first time I experienced worship with hundreds of other Christians. I began to feel more liberated in my worship, clapping my hands, raising my arms, jigging up and down to the music. During these times, I found myself making sounds that were not in English, expressing the love I felt in my heart for Jesus. I learned this was praying or singing in the Spirit and I used this in my prayer life, whether praying on my own or with others.

It was at one of these conferences that I received a promise from God. One of the speakers addressed those of us in the congregation who were experiencing difficulties in our marriages. He said he believed that our marriages could be healed and prayed for us by encouraging us to ask God ourselves for the healing that was needed. As I stood with others, and with my friends who knew my situation around me supporting me in prayer, I made my own request as follows:

My marriage would be healed by Keith coming back;
Keith would become a Christian;
Our relationship would be better than before.

With the speaker leading us in prayer and with many witnesses standing with me, I believed that God heard my prayer and would answer it. It took thirteen years but all three parts of that promise have been fulfilled. This is why I know God is a faithful God and will never let me down.

I had learned that I could not change Keith. I had to surrender him to Jesus and pray His will into Keith's life. The person I could change was myself and this is what I did with the help of Jesus and my new-found church.

Two-and-a-half years and many highs and lows later found me older and hopefully wiser. It was May 1992 and I was praying one day, reading from Psalm 40. Verse 6 says: 'Sacrifice and offering you did not desire, but my ears you have pierced.' This reminded me of the ancient tradition relating to slaves and masters. If a master offered a slave his freedom, but the slave refused to take it as he loved his master and did not want to leave his service, then the master would pierce the slave's ear to show the slave had freely chosen to remain a servant. This led me to pray: 'If Keith coming back means I do not need You as much, then keep Keith away.' Considering that Keith coming back into the marriage had been my heart's prayer for the last two to three years, this was a brave prayer to say, but I meant it. The very next evening, the doorbell rang. Keith stood on the doorstep, unexpectedly, and said: 'I cannot not have another go at our marriage. I want to move back in.' Then, true to his sense of timing and occasion, he added: 'I realise this is short notice, so if you don't want me to come back tonight, then I could move back tomorrow morning.'

The first part of God's threefold promise had been fulfilled. Keith moved back home after two-and-a-half years' separation. In October of that year, just three years after the breakdown of our relationship, he too discovered Jesus for himself and became a full member of the church that had sustained the girls and myself. The second part of the promise had happened.

The third part was that our marriage would be better than it had been before. This took a lot longer as we had to work through many difficulties, build up trust once again and learn to share our deepest and most personal thoughts and feelings. But that too came and now, having celebrated more than thirty years of marriage, we can sincerely say that our marriage is the best it has ever been.

People who have heard my testimony, Christians and others, tell me that it is so unusual for a marriage to suffer such a long period of separation and yet be fully healed. I have met no one else for whom this has happened, although I am sure there are some. That is why I believe that it was the divine intervention of a loving and all-powerful God that brought about this miracle. This is why, whenever I now encounter difficulties in my life, my first response is to pray to Jesus and to trust Him to work through these difficulties with me. I do not know how long it will take to see answers in some of these situations but I do know that I serve a faithful God who will never let me down and who knows what is best for me. I can trust Him because He loves me and is completely committed to me. The only adequate response from me is a total commitment to Him. I am so thankful that God never gave up trying to communicate with me.

My Business is God's Business

As dark and rugged as his wife, Zena, is fair and delicately feminine, Vince Von-Rollock makes up one half of a visually striking couple. Blessed with arresting looks, this duo's external appearance only serves to enhance their inner integrity and spiritual maturity. When Vince speaks, he doesn't hold back, he tells it as it is. But his words carry the weight of a personal transformation developed and honed over the years through his experiences and knowledge of God. With her keen mind, Zena can offer astute insights and wisdom into perplexing situations and has proved herself a valuable and trustworthy friend to those who know her. Both acutely business-minded, they have together built up many lucrative ventures over the years, their respective strengths complementing each other. Yet it is primarily Vince's testimony which forms the focus of this section. The reason for this will become clear as his testimony unfolds.

Barbados-born Vince was born into poverty in 1955. He was raised by his church-going grandmother in northern St Lucy, while his parents lived and worked in Bridgetown, St Michael, at the southern end of the island, to support their family. He firmly believes that his early upbringing shaped his future destiny. 'I have some tremendous memories of going to church with my grandma,' he says. 'Anything that's really happened to me personally, in the spiritual realm, I really believe is as a result of my grandma's input.'

This dedicated lady would regularly usher her young grandson to evening church services where a sleepy Vince would doze contentedly, lulled into slumber by the steady tattoo of rain on the galvanised roof. 'She made sure I went to Sunday School,' he says. 'And I had a good spiritual upbringing. I can remember almost all of my Sunday School teachers. I can remember that if we arrived late, rather than walking straight in, we had to kneel and say a prayer before we sat down. Just reflecting on that, that was quite nice. We had a lot of Bible studies.' The church encouraged its youngsters to take an active part in the services and Vince was asked to bring a word to the congregation at the age of nine. 'And that was the first time I ever preached,' he recalls.

Vince believes that God had a definite purpose for his life as, looking back, he remembers several occasions when his life should have ended. The first of these incidents occurred at the age of eleven. 'The West Indies is affected by storms and hurricanes at certain times of the year,' he explains. 'And we had just experienced a small hurricane.' Knowing that her grandson loved nothing better than going for a swim at the nearby beach, his grandmother warned him not to venture out that day as the stormy conditions meant that this activity would be highly dangerous. With the impetuosity of youth, however, as soon as he saw his chance to slip out of the dwelling unnoticed, he headed for his favourite bay, all exhortations to the contrary unheeded.

'And I was out in the sea swimming and playing with my friends,' he goes on. 'We were at Chandler's Bay, which was safe to swim in as the water was very low. But next to Chandler's Bay was Maycocks Bay and story had it that it was bottomless. In reality, it was so deep that only adult men and strong swimmers would go in. It was also very rough with a strong undercurrent. I was playing nearby. I thought I could swim but couldn't really and went out a little bit too far. All of a sudden I just felt myself being pulled away. I knew I was drowning because I kept going up and down and drinking a lot of water and it was one of the first times in my life that I thought about death.' Curiously, amid all this panic, Vince felt a deep peace and prepared to surrender himself to the inevitable. Suddenly, he spotted a friend in the water nearby. Although he was not much older than Vince, this adolescent – a serial truant who spent the best part of every day in the sea – was an exceptionally strong swimmer. 'He was really fantastic. I remember shouting and waving at him to let him know that I was in difficulty. When he swam closer, I grabbed hold of him, which is the worst thing to do when somebody's trying to save you. I remember him shouting and swearing at me, asking me to get off him.' And then, realising that his message was not getting across to his struggling companion: 'He gave me a couple of punches in the head, he really did.' The two finally reached the safety of the shore and a relieved Vince set off home only to face the wrath of his grandmother and 'one of the worst beatings of my life'.

Unnerved by this near-disaster and fearing for the safety of her young charge, Vince's grandmother wrote to his mother explaining what had happened. By this time his parents had emigrated to England and decided that the best course of action would be for Vince to come and live with them.

As a twelve-year old, Vince's first impressions of the country were not favourable. 'I thought England was going to be this tremendous country. As kids we had heard so much about England and I knew that my mum had gone there to have a better lifestyle.' Life in Barbados had been tough: living in a shack, going to school without shoes, sometimes going to bed without any food, and using eating utensils fashioned from whatever materials were readily available – halved fruit husks for bowls and old tin cans for cups. And yet to the young boy, it seemed that life in 1960s' England was not much better.

For the first time in his young life, Vince encountered racial prejudice in the form of taunts and name-calling at his new school. He remembers that his family also felt unwelcome at the local church and so restricted their attendance to a twice yearly visit at Christmas and Easter with the predominantly black Seventh Day Adventists.

As soon as he could, Vince left school, by his own admission 'without any education at all' and joined the Army. Completing his initial training in Wales, he was posted to Northern Ireland. 'And again,' he states. 'This is how I am absolutely convinced that God's hand was on my life, no ifs, no buts. While we were on active service in Ireland, there were maybe two occasions when I should have died and my life was preserved by God. He definitely had His hand on me, even though I wasn't a Christian back then.

'One thing is, I never liked people ordering me about, and I shouldn't have been in the Army because I couldn't take orders. What happened was that one of the leaders in charge of our section, a corporal with whom I shared a room, asked me to do something and I refused. "There's other people here," I told him. "I've been working. I'm not doing it." I never had problems mucking in, but if I was mucking in, others had to muck in as well. He started saying that he was going to take me to be charged by the military section so I knocked the stuffing out of him. You're not supposed to lay your hand on your superiors and I did. The thing is I could have got court-martialled, I could have got jailed,

I could have got thrown out of the Army but he never said a word. There were officers there who had heard what had gone on but he absolutely refused to press charges or to discuss what had happened. They knew I was responsible for it and he said: "I just fell against one of the lockers." And either that night or the next we were in the canteen and I got absolutely drunk. Out of my senses. Couldn't walk, couldn't talk. I stumbled back to my room. I wasn't aware of what was going on once I got to bed but I was comatose and vomiting. I could have choked and died that night but for the corporal who I'd just levelled a couple of days earlier. And I mean this guy, he came in and woke me up; I heard him shout: "Come on! Let's help this man. He's going to die if we don't look after him." And he cleaned up all my vomit, changed all my bedding, undressed me, took me to the showers and showered me down. He put some clean clothes back on me and stood guard over me all night to make sure that I was OK.'

Remembering this episode, Vince, visibly moved, cannot continue with his narrative. When he can speak he says: 'Honestly, if it was me that had just got levelled and I saw the guy there dying … at the time I think I'd have finished me off. And when I look back, I just think that was an act of Christian kindness, wasn't it? He wasn't a black guy, he was a white guy and he was lovely.'

On another occasion, his unit was out on location with the Marines in sniper territory when a sudden shouted command to get down caused an already agitated Vince to instead stand to his feet in shock. A prime target directly in the line of fire, he had to be forcibly dragged down by one of his comrades. The weapons trained on him missed their mark and he lived to tell the tale. 'Definitely God preserved me because I shouldn't be here,' he declares.

His next posting was to Germany where he became a physical training instructor. At this time, discrimination again reared its head. He remembers on one occasion being denied entrance to a club: 'You're black. You can't come in here.' Experiences such as this were not uncommon and Vince admits that at the time they shaped him psychologically. Indeed, they were the motivating factor behind some serious but ill-thought out decisions.

He got involved with a young girl from a white family. Unfortunately her parents, when they found out, did not approve of their daughter's choice of boyfriend and were worried about the possibility of a marriage. Up until that point, Vince had not even considered the question of matrimony but their stance provoked him into proposing. His girlfriend accepted and the two soon became man and wife. 'It was stupidity really,' he acknowledges. In time the couple were able to announce the arrival of a beautiful baby boy. Sadly, but perhaps predictably, the marriage built on its rocky foundation did not last and Vince returned to England alone.

On leaving the Army he suffered much discouragement in his search for a civilian job but eventually was appointed to a post in his chosen sector – sales. Discovering a natural aptitude in this field, he quickly progressed up the career ladder, winning awards along the way, and moved into management. It was at this stage in 1986, while working in Barnsley, a small Yorkshire town, that Zena walked into his life. 'And she worked as a sales person and then she worked as my secretary ... she was absolutely beautiful.' Vince was totally captivated. Both were in relationships at the time but eventually ended them in favour of each other. Although neither were church-goers or committed to any faith, he maintains that they were both God-conscious and would spend most of their time talking about their Creator. Very quickly their relationship deepened. They became an established couple and married. Life seemed good. 'I was making so much money,' Vince says. 'I bought Zena a Porsche and I drove Bentleys, Mercedes, the full business. It was incredible and money was coming out of our ears.'

Then, in 1988, Vince started to experience agonising neck and chest pains. X-rays revealed a collapsed lung and the young man suddenly feared for the future. It was then that he remembered the number. The previous year he had attended a business meeting in America. Retiring to bed after a long day's work, he was jolted awake in the early hours by a voice urging him to: 'Turn the television on.' Startled, he obeyed the command and was instantly met by a scenario of sick and disabled people apparently being healed. A television evangelist was conducting a service and people were getting out of their wheelchairs exclaiming that they had been cured of their infirmities. Watching the scene, Vince was sceptical. 'I thought it was just a load of nonsense, you know. It thought it was manipulation and I didn't fully believe it.' As the programme was drawing to a close, however, the flickering screen displayed a prayer line telephone number which the viewing audience was encouraged to contact in the event of any unresolved problems. 'I took down the number,' Vince says. 'Don't ask me why, I just took it, put it in my briefcase and went back to sleep.'

Now he reached for his business folders, retrieved the slip of paper and dialled. After explaining his predicament, he was assured by the woman's voice on the other end of the line that it is not God's intention for anyone to suffer from sickness and disease. This lady then prayed for him, her intercession carrying across the miles from a call centre in America to a home in the north of England. At the time Vince asserts that he did not feel any lightning bolts or anything approximating a supernatural happening, but in his need he sent up a heartfelt prayer of his own: 'God, if you can prove Yourself to me, I will do whatever it takes to live a life that would be in accordance with Your Word.'

The following day, Vince turned up for his scheduled appointment at the health clinic. After examining his chest, the doctor redirected him to the hospital for his next set of X-rays. Once there, the images produced from the electromagnetic waves showed a clear reversal of the previous situation. His lungs were now perfectly healthy. The physician was nonplussed. 'I don't know what's happened here,' he said. 'But your lungs have healed back up.' Vince answered him with a new-found surety that a prayer uttered over the telephone had been instrumental in his recovery. 'And the doctor didn't acknowledge or try to discredit it,' says Vince. He said, "Prayer can sometimes work".'

At the time all this was taking place, both Vince and Zena were experiencing a growing dissatisfaction with their lives. Materially, they had everything they could wish for and yet they felt a lack of something indefinable. Amid all their success, they knew something was missing. 'I definitely wanted to invite God in so He could help us out,' Vince remembers. This wealthy man now earnestly and continuously prayed for God to reveal Himself to him. God always shows Himself faithful to those who seek Him. In Revelation 3:20 Jesus says: 'Here I am! I stand at the door and knock. If anyone hears my voice and opens the door, I will come in and eat with him, and he with me.' Vince's entreaties were about to be answered in a unique and dramatic way.

One night, soon after sending up his heartfelt pleas, he woke to behold what he describes as a ball of fire in his bedroom. Realising that this was no ordinary blaze as no destruction was evident in its wake, Vince felt the flames conveying their powerful message straight into his spirit: 'I am God, and I want you in a relationship with me.' Throughout the Bible, God's Holy Spirit has appeared in this form to the awestruck wonder of those to whom He chose to reveal Himself (Exodus 3:2; Exodus 13.21: Exodus 19:18; Acts 2:3). Hebrews 12:29 refers to God as a 'consuming fire'. He is the same yesterday, today and tomorrow and as He worked in the past, so He continues to work in the present, as Vince's experience bears witness to. This symbol of God's presence was to continue to manifest itself over a number of nights, heralding the start of a new and extraordinary spiritual awakening.

The couple had started to attend a church and the pastor, having spoken to Vince briefly, visited them at home for a more in-depth discourse. It was to prove a pivotal and life-changing encounter. The problems that the couple were experiencing were discussed from a Biblical perspective. The clergyman pointed to scriptures which held the key to the issues they had been grappling with and suddenly it all seemed to make sense. 'And he was just talking,' Vince says. 'And I looked up to the corner of the ceiling and there I saw before me ... I can't describe it but if I could, I would say that I saw the wind. I mean, how do you see the wind? But that's what I saw, I saw the wind. And this wind had the appearance of a cloak. I stood up and I heard this thing, that looked like the wind that had the appearance of a cloak, say to me: "I am the Holy Spirit and it's your turn for a visitation from me tonight." I felt sick, I felt horrible, I felt as though I was going to die at that moment and I said to the pastor: "I don't really want to hear any more," and he just put his hand straight on my head and started praying. And while he was praying for me I had the experience that I was dying and feeling helpless and lost. He then started to pray: "Lord Jesus, we bring Vincent to the Cross. And Lord we bring him to the Cross, not to live, but to die." And as he said that, I fell to the floor and I wasn't accustomed to seeing people falling on the floor, so it wasn't something that I'd practised. But I remember falling to the floor and all sorts of experiences were going through my body at the time. It felt to me as though I had gone back in time through eternity and that I was at the Crucifixion. I felt Jesus on the Cross above me. I also felt as though I was being born again. I felt as though I was coming out of the birth canal, I absolutely felt it. I don't know how long the experience lasted but I remember the pastor praying for me. I had never heard any person pray like that before. It was very authoritative. It was different and it was all in the name of Jesus. How long it lasted, I don't know. What I do know is that after he had finished praying I felt clean. I felt as though I had been dipped into some kind of purifying water and I felt scrubbed and I felt wonderful. And I sat down on the sofa and I remember he asked me, "How do you feel?" And I started crying as though I was a baby, as though I had just been born. "I feel as though I've just been born," I said. And he went on: "Well, being born again is biblical, you know." "But you don't understand," I said, "I thought I was dying." He explained that it was biblical, that the old self had been put to death. ('For we know that our old self was crucified with him so that the body of sin might be done away with, that we should no longer be slaves to sin' Romans 6:6). And I read the Scriptures afterwards and it made sense. So two things happened to me: the old nature was put to death, no ifs, no buts. The sinful nature was absolutely slain that night. And not only that, I was born again. And when I read that scripture now where Nicodemus is talking to Jesus about being born again (John 3: 1-8), I know what being 'born again' is. And I became born again on 8 May 1989 at 9.30 in the evening.'

At the time, Zena, who had left the two men to what was ostensibly a religious discussion, was unaware of the drama unfolding in the next room. Vince's encounter with God, however, led to her own salvation two nights later. She simply telephoned the pastor and the two prayed together, asking God to forgive her sins and thanking His Son for dying on the Cross, so taking her punishment. Polar opposites in their intensity, the couple's experiences shared the same outcome: a spiritual rebirth and the promise of salvation. 'Zena didn't have the same dramatic experience that I had, but I suppose I needed it,' says Vince. 'I needed convincing.'

The couple threw themselves into their new-found relationship with God. This proved so radical and all-encompassing that they immediately questioned the fundamentals of their life up until that point. Within the week they had made the decision to shut down their profitable sales business. 'Not that it was illegal,' explains Vince. 'It was a good, honest business.' But with his new spiritual sensitivity, he recognised that the nature of the work meant that ethics were being compromised and for both of them, this was no longer an option.

This courageous step of faith bore fruit and Vince has since gone on to become a successful motivational speaker, running worldwide seminars for executives in all professions. He takes no credit, however, for his undoubted talent in this field. 'That's not me, that's God,' he pronounces. 'I am amazed at how God can take a little black boy from Barbados with no education, no shoes … honestly, can hardly put two words together. I mean, what have I got in common with a scientist or a doctor? Absolutely nothing. That's the favour of God. It really is.'

Over the years he has been asked to preach at many meetings. A close Christian walk (relationship with God) and study of the Scriptures has given him a direct insight into the truth and power held within God's word. On one occasion, while speaking about God's ability to heal, something incredible started to happen. Unknown to Vince, a lady who suffered from curvature of the spine was in the congregation, and as she listened to the message suddenly her body started rotating and she straightened up. Her doctors, when they subsequently examined her, could offer no rational explanation. It seemed that medical science could not account for the change in this woman's physical make-up. 'That's just God's word,' says Vince. 'When we preach God's word, that's what happens.'

In Psalm 107:20 we read that: 'He sent forth his word and healed them, he rescued them from the grave.' The Bible is described as the living word of God. As such, it is holy and breathes 'wholeness' or health into our lives. Indeed, the origin of the word 'holy' is *halig*, which is related to *whole*.[3] We can, and should, expect changes when we delve into this most sacred manuscript.

---

3 Pearsall J (Ed) (2002) *Concise Oxford English Dictionary* 10th Edition Revised, Oxford University Press

In the afore-mentioned incident, a physical healing was the result of the imparting of God's word. On another occasion, the healing of psychological and emotional wounds restored wholeness to a hurting and frightened young woman. It happened in Macedonia where he had been invited, along with his pastor, to the home of a Greek pastor. One morning, he woke up early and got down on his knees to pray. 'And I was praying,' he says. 'Suddenly I saw something like a cinema screen in front of me and it was like I was at the pictures. I saw this girl running away from people and being cornered. I continued to pray and asked: "What's this God?" and I heard God say to me: "You're going to see this woman tonight. She's been hurt a lot. Christians, or people who call themselves Christians, have abused her and I'm going to set her free from this tonight."'

God then revealed how this girl had been sexually abused, leaving her feeling ashamed and struggling to come to terms with what had happened. 'I just prayed,' continues Vince. 'And I asked God to heal and restore her'.

Later in the day he was asked by his host to bring a word to the evening service. It was a last-minute decision, totally unplanned. 'And as I was at the meeting, this woman walked into the room and something in my chest went like that,' Vince says. With his hands, he illustrates his heart seeming to twist and click. 'And I said, 'What's that?' and God said: "That's the woman I showed you in your vision this morning." I preached the word and the meeting came to an end.' As the service was drawing to a close, however, he conveyed to the pastor's wife his belief that he had been given a message for a specific person in the gathering. Understanding from Vince's comments that this could be a difficult or sensitive issue, she suggested that they lead the young woman to a quiet area of the church where they could minister to her undisturbed. 'So we guided her out to the vestry,' Vince goes on. 'And I shared with her what God had showed me. And this is when you know it's God, because she looked at me and confirmed that it was all true and she was crying. Then she said: "Well, this is strange because I was working today and God gave me a vision of a black man. I wasn't coming here, it was a last minute thing" She added that God had told her: "That person is going to pray for you tonight and you're going to be free."

'Don't tell me that God's not real,' Vince asserts. 'He is, you know. And she got freed! She really did.'

We can know, therefore, that God sees our sufferings and pain and can step in to release us from their bondage. Sometimes, however, it would appear that a sought-for healing has not taken place, at least in our eyes. At such times it would be easy and all too human to assume that nothing supernatural had happened and that God had not stepped in to resolve the situation. And yet God is God. In Jeremiah 1:5 He says: 'Before I formed you in the womb I knew you.' He alone knows us intimately, He knew us before we were conceived, He knows us better than our families and loved ones. Better, even, than ourselves. It follows, then, that His perfect will may not coincide with ours, as He alone has complete understanding of every situation and we may never fully comprehend His reasoning until we meet Him face to face in eternity. Vince shares poignantly his own beloved sister's battle with cancer. Up until she was diagnosed with the disease, this younger sibling had been a follower of a movement which taught that a male born in the twentieth century was a manifestation of

God or the Son of God. As this woman lay dying of a malignant tumour in her breast, Vince spoke to her of the truths held in the Bible. 'The long and short of it all is that eventually after speaking to her, I told her that I loved her very much and that I would never lie to her' he says. 'And she accepted the Lord. I was really happy about that and was aware that God could now heal her. She started to get better and then she started to go back to the same things that God had just saved her from.' The cancer returned, this time claiming her life. 'And I asked God this question when she died: "God, why is my sister dead? She's only thirty-nine. She accepted you." You know what? God showed me a picture. He showed me His hand, and He showed my sister in His hand and Jesus said to me: "Those that the Father has given to me, no-one can pluck away. If I didn't bring your sister home, she would have been influenced and been taken away back into the world. That's why, when I had her there, I said: 'Come home.'"

'And I can cope with that,' states Vince. 'I really can.'

What we may perceive in our pain and confusion as defeat, God claims as a glorious victory. His ultimate plan is to bring us safely home and He had allowed this distraught brother a glimpse into His divine purpose and will. Of his sister, Vince says: 'When she closed her eyes, she was healed. She really was. But not only was she healed, she was in the presence of the Lord. Of course I grieve for my sister. Of course there are times when I cry about her, but I have comfort in the fact that God showed up and spoke to me and told me: "Hey, she's with me. Don't worry about it." And I've said to Zena on many occasions: "She'll not come back here, but we'll go forward and see her".'

Vince's close relationship with God has shaped the man he has now become. His relationship with the son he left behind in Germany has been restored and he is a passionate family man. The year before he submitted his testimony he embarked on a new business venture together with his wife, the profits of which are intended to be channelled into areas of need within their own local community and further afield. 'This one's not for us,' Vince states. 'This is for God, this one.'

And no-one can argue with that.

My Quest for Peace

It's not that I went off the rails exactly. I wouldn't call regular cannabis use and recreational harder drug consumption 'off the rails' but it nearly sent me careering off the track nevertheless.

I started smoking cannabis at the age of fifteen, me and a friend smoking with her boyfriend, if he had any. By the time I was sixteen I was buying my own. Any spare money from the allowance my parents gave me, or from summer work, went on alcohol, cigarettes and draw (cannabis). The trouble is, when you start chasing 'highs' you're always trying to get to your next one. Life in the middle is either running off your last one or building up to your next and you start experimenting with other things just to see how they'll affect you. For me, once I'd stepped over that 'it's against the law' barrier, there were no more holds barred and when I was offered other drugs like speed and coke, I didn't hesitate. Even LSD, after a little persuading from friends, was on my regularly consumed 'menu'. Anything and everything with the exception of heroin. Heroin had, and still has I think, a bit of a social taboo even among regular drug users. Heroin users and addicts tend to be excluded and therefore run on a separate social circuit.

Anyway, that's how my teenage years passed, literally in a drug induced haze, 'up in smoke'. Let me say at this point that I wasn't an abused child. I didn't come from a deprived or poverty-stricken background. I didn't, in fact, lack for anything in my home life. I was a much loved, supported daughter to parents who were still together and still in love with one another. It's just that I couldn't accept that that's all there was to life. To get a job, work hard, fall in love, get married, have kids. There had to be more surely? Surely there was more! Drugs was my answer. Here was more. Here was a whole level of reality. I honestly considered non-drug users to be seriously missing out.

By the time I was nineteen, I began to want more – not more drugs, you understand, but more to my life. I wanted to *do* more with it, to see more of it, expand my horizons if you will. So I began to look for work which would take me abroad. Subscribing to a job search magazine, I began my hunt. The trouble was, I didn't have enough qualifications. I mean, I had some O-levels (precursors to today's GCSEs), and had scraped through A-levels, but nothing vocational. Still I carried on looking, convinced that travel was in my blood, having spent my formative years in Hong Kong. I came across an advert for a 'gaming academy' in London who, for a fee of several hundred pounds, offered to train you in a couple of casino games, guaranteeing you work abroad on the cruise lines. This sounded great to me and I made all the necessary enquiries.

During the process of application I saw in the local newspaper that a nearby casino was advertising to recruit personnel and train them in two games. They were offering a small wage for the training with an increase on completion. 'What's the catch?' I thought, but there wasn't one. I applied, trained successfully, and worked in that casino for a year before I attended a recruitment day held by a major cruise line in the gaming academy in London. Months later I was flying out to Miami to be assigned to a ship, then over to LA to join it.

I worked on the cruise lines for almost four years; four different ships and several runs, visiting some of the most beautiful islands in the world: Grenada, St Lucia, Virgin Gorda. Many, many beautiful places. I earned, and spent, a lot of money in my time away. A young woman, wages cash in hand, no tax, no board and no bills. I'm painting a luxurious and idyllic picture here. Don't get me wrong, it was hard work on the ships: six days a week, split shifts. Work, eat, sleep, with the same people, only speaking to family and friends by telephone in cramped call station booths … but the pleasures, the pleasures were extreme too. It was definitely a time, a season in my life which could be described as living hard, playing hard. Crew members had their own bar in which drinks were extremely cheap, so drinking to excess was almost a nightly occurrence. And don't think for a moment that my travelling to new climes had abated my drug use. Oh, no. Now I could get drugs from closer to their source: cannabis from Jamaica, cocaine from Puerto Rico. It was never difficult to get hold of whatever whim or fancy might be on the 'want list' of the moment. So this was my lifestyle for about four years. Working hard, yes, but living life's extremes. Friends and lovers from all over the world. Sex, drugs and rock and roll, except rock and roll never was my scene! Don't get me wrong, I don't want to glorify these things. They aren't they shouldn't be what anyone's life revolves around. But to pretend that it was all dark and sordid, depraved and seedy, would be a lie. I enjoyed the life I was living. It was fun, and I had some exceptionally good times in those years, and though I am not proud of the things I did or the way I behaved, the experience has shaped and moulded me into who I am today.

What I do want to emphasise about this part of my life is that despite the fact that I was living life to excess, I was never really satisfied, and deep down I knew none of this held any value. They were 'good times', yes, but they were superficial and shallow, unfulfilling and worthless.

I began wondering what to do with my life now? Where to go and what to do when I got there? I knew I'd had enough of the ship life, so I ended up going back to where I'd come from, which was Cardiff. I got my old job back, moved in with an old friend and just got right on back into the life I'd left there. But going backwards was never going to work. Before I'd been there with hopes and dreams, with ambitions and goals, now I had none. I had no sense of direction for, or in, my life and as a result felt dead, mundane, lifeless. I became despondent and then depressed.

I continued to smoke my cannabis during this dark period of my life and this exacerbated the problem and my depression became very deep. I would hide away in my room for days on end. I came out to go to work, to score my draw, to do those things I had to do, but they became a real ordeal for me. I was becoming a real sociophobe. The thought of spending time with people, anyone, filled me with dread and fear. I could barely tolerate my own company. I would lie in my room deriding myself for feeling the way I was feeling, knowing there were no physical circumstances or logical reason for it, and being disgusted with myself for behaving in this way. This, as I say, was a dark, dark, period of my life. It was, however, one for which I'm eternally grateful. It was through this season of despair that I began to cry out, began to search for a way out, to seek a light to inspire, to guide me through. I was convinced that this was a spiritual journey and that it was 'spiritual' healing that I needed. A family member had been involved in a spiritualist church and I knew they prayed healing prayers for people, so I looked in the Yellow Pages for the local spiritualist church. I went along to find out where it was. They had a poster in the window advertising a healing prayer meeting the next day. I was excited at the prospect and went home to my room determined to go along the following evening.

Now, my friend who I shared a flat with was a Rastafarian and knowing my predicament she'd given me a Bible, sections of which Rastas adhere to. She encouraged me to read Job and the Psalms. So that evening I'd gone home and picked up my Bible, which was becoming a regular thing for me, and for some reason read Deuteronomy 18:11-12 which warns against being a spiritualist or medium. For obvious reasons this had an impact on me. It was as if I was walking down a path and had strode headlong into a concrete barrier – stopped, knocked back on my butt. No further progression on this path possible. I'd obviously got it wrong, but where to look now?

During one of my many visits to the library, I picked up a book by a lady called Jackie Pullinger called *Chasing the Dragon*[4], which was about her work with heroin addicts inside the walled city in Hong Kong. Obviously the drug and Hong Kong connection appealed to me, so I booked it out and took it home. The book gripped me, which was remarkable enough on its own because since the start of my depression, no book other than the Bible had been able to hold my attention. But this Jackie Pullinger book was different. I was, as I say, gripped. In the book I read about addicts being freed from their addiction through the power of prayer to Jesus Christ. One day they were shooting up smack, the next day they were totally changed: believers in Jesus and filled with the Holy Spirit. The book referred to this 'filling with the Holy Spirit' a lot and also 'praying in tongues'. I'd heard of this before and didn't know what was meant by it but my curiosity was perked. Here was a God who actually intervened in people's

---

4   Pullinger, Jackie with Quicke, Andrew (2006) *Chasing the Dragon*, Hodder and Stoughton

lives. He wasn't far off and distant, just accepting songs of praise from His people on Sundays but other than that not playing any part in their lives. He was real, He was radical and I wanted to know more, so I began ringing around churches in the area asking them if they worshipped 'in the Spirit' and 'spoke in tongues'. As I say, I had very little understanding of what this meant, but I did know, from what I'd read, it was being filled with the 'Holy Spirit' and 'praying in tongues' which preceded breakthrough in the heroin addicts' lives.

Anyway, I got a variety of responses from churches but eventually, through a Christian Student Union directory, I found a church with 'spirit-filled worship'. I rang them and was told they'd be delighted for me to come along on Sunday. So I did. I was made to feel very welcome there and, although socialising was still extremely difficult for me, I kept attending. I was still reading my Bible at home and everything being taught at the church confirmed what I was reading. But I was still very, very low. I was convinced this was the right track, but the practicalities of day to day life were still very hard to deal with, so I decided to approach the pastor of the church with a scripture I'd found: 'Is any one of you sick? He should call the elders of the church to pray over him and anoint him with oil in the name of the Lord' (James 5:14). I wrote this scripture out and put it in my pocket ready to speak to the pastor at the end of the service. The end of the service came and I couldn't pluck up the courage to go and speak to him, I was too scared. At this point, the pastor got up and said that we were going to do something a little different this morning and what he would like to do was to pray for people. He proceeded to read out the self same scripture which was written out on the paper in my pocket. He said that if anyone needed prayer they were to come to the front of the church. I did and he prayed for me. I don't remember if I was asked what I needed prayer for, but I do know that from that day a radical change happened within me. I know the pastor prayed for me to be filled with the Holy Spirit and although I didn't fully understand what that meant, I absolutely knew that I was not the same as I had been. There were physical symptoms. I had flashing in my peripheral vision, I was excited, adrenaline was pumping through my body. I felt alive, having felt dead for the previous six months. I really felt alive, perhaps more alive than I'd ever felt. I was working an afternoon shift at the casino after the service and as I was leaving, the pastor encouraged me to try and speak 'in tongues'. He told me I wouldn't understand what I was saying and I'd probably think I was making it up, but just to trust it was God working in me. As I was walking to work I began to pray in this 'tongues' language and I continued under my breath throughout the afternoon at work. I now understand that this language is the Holy Spirit living inside me and praying through me. It is a gift from God, one which lifts our spirit, and for which I am extremely grateful.

When I got home that evening, my Rastafarian friend could see a difference in me. She could see that something about me had changed. She put it down to a 'religious experience' and in a sense she was right. But I don't think she could begin to understand the difference that experience had made in my life; the difference that Jesus made to my attitudes, to my thought processes, to my behaviour.

I am writing this ten years on and sadly have lost touch with her. Happily, God continues to work in our lives throughout our Christian walk and He has continued to work changes in me. Within ten months of the pastor praying for me, I'd quit my job in the casino, knowing for sure that God didn't want me in that environment. I'd quit smoking, not just dope but cigarettes as well and I no longer swore. Let me emphasise that, in my experience, none of these things were conscious decisions; they were just a consequence of my continued relationship with God. I moved away from Cardiff and my old lifestyle and started attending Huddersfield Christian Fellowship. My former pastor recommended the church, which his friend, Colin Cooper, pastored.

I've been attending now for over nine years. God has given me many opportunities to grow, to expand my horizons and travel in my time here. I've travelled to Africa, Romania and America doing His work, which, believe me, is a far greater experience than visiting these places merely as a tourist. I've been interviewed on live Christian television, which, strangely, is what my casino manager predicted in Cardiff, and have generally benefited tremendously from being a member of the family that is Huddersfield Christian Fellowship. Most importantly, the life I now live is fulfilled. Don't get me wrong, life can seem pretty mundane at times, but gone is the gaping hole in my life which all my hard living had failed to satisfy. It is filled with an assurance, a peace, an absolute certainly that the path I'm now on is the right one. It is a literal experience of being born again into a whole new lifestyle, attitude and perspective. My life, formerly of no consequence, now, because it belongs to God, is consequential.

'Would you like this to happen to other little girls?'

She follows him into the small apartment. Delighted that she's met such a thoughtful friend who flatters her with his attention and little gifts, she feels safe and entirely at ease with him. But she is only seven, and he an adult male …

'I was on holiday with my parents and sister in Spain,' Hannah begins. 'There was a man there the caretaker of the apartments where we were staying. He started to slowly entice me to befriend him and I thought he was my friend. He began to give me little presents and after a few days of this he started to sexually abuse me. He didn't speak any English but he spoke Spanish to me quite strongly which, when I look back now, made me feel quite scared, so I'm sure it was something like: "Don't tell anybody about this," or "This is our secret," because of the tone of his voice. Some people in the neighbouring apartment realised something funny was going on and mentioned it to my dad. I remember that he took me aside and gently asked what was happening with this man. I burst into tears and he tried to comfort me, telling me that it wasn't my fault, because that had been my initial reaction: it was my fault – I was the one in the wrong. I didn't want to go to the police to testify against this man because he had scared me into keeping quiet. But my dad said to me: "Do you want him to do this to other little girls?" and it was that that stuck with me and inspired me to give evidence against him.

'After that it was all shut away for a period of time until I started to grow up. I don't recall ever speaking to my parents or family about it. I didn't feel the need to go into detail about what had happened because that would have been horrific. However, anything that was mentioned about sexual abuse or rape, or anything of a sexual nature would kind of twang at my heart. It was a hidden pain, no one knew about it because I kept it quiet. But certain things, like the smell of cigars (because he used to smoke them) would trigger off flashbacks and as I got older these increased. Also, I hated being near anyone who would see my body. I didn't like my body. I didn't like anybody looking at me or touching me. I didn't realise that it stemmed from the sexual abuse, I just thought it was me as a person.

'When I was sixteen I was in a bit of a bad way. I had a job but I was on the drugs Ecstasy and speed, which I was taking daily and I'd gone down to seven-and-a-half stones, very skinny and pale. I'm not built to be skinny so it was noticeable. My parents regularly tried to find out what was the matter with me but I never said that there was anything wrong. I was like ten moody teenagers rolled into one! Once when they were away I held a party and my brother-in-law, who is a Christian, walked in on what I was doing. I wasn't just taking speed, I was selling it and it was a lot deeper. I had got myself into a mess. He told my parents and I thought that this was it – they'd stop loving me and kick me out because I'd let them down. But, of course, when they found out they just wanted to sort me out. They wanted to help me. We were a Christian family and they told me that the way I was living wasn't what God wanted for me and suggested that I go to a Bible College in Ireland. At that point, I realised that I wanted to stop the drugs and move away. I knew I couldn't stay at home and move my life on because of the influence of my friends. I'm a very easily-led person so I wouldn't have been able to say "no".

Hannah's foray into Bible-based vocational training lasted only four months, an outcome she attributes to her misguided motivation in entering the college. 'I was thrown out,' she states simply. 'I believe it was because I went there for the wrong reasons. I wanted to be protected from the world and I thought, naïvely, that there wouldn't be any temptation there.' She had made a commitment to God at the age of six but a few months after this latest episode, in her own words, she 'fell away from God completely'. However, the short time spent there resulted in Hannah's first breakthrough. 'It was in my "quiet time,"' she recalls. 'I was reading the Book of Psalms when I had a revelation that God could heal my hurts, my pain. He could stop my flashbacks and memories. He had the power to erase my memory of the abuse. That Sunday we had our usual meeting and the sermon was about forgiving and forgetting, about God healing our minds and our hearts. I went to the front for prayer. I wanted more than anything to forget the face of the man who had sexually abused me. It had haunted me for long enough and knowing what the Word of God says, I believed that God would "erase" the memory of this man's face. And He did! I left that meeting not being able to remember his face, and here I am at twenty-six, I still can't remember it. It just vanished. I can't picture it or place it. Ten years of nightmares and flashbacks with this man's face and God took it away in an instant. I can still recall what happened to me but I can't remember his face.'

This development, Hannah's first step in her quest for inner peace, was followed by the more conventional route of psychiatric analysis, a course of action which left her perplexed. 'I only had one session with the psychiatrist and it involved me talking about the sexual abuse in as much detail as I could. I spoke, he listened. He asked questions, I answered. I can't recall any advice being given or any help being offered. I didn't feel any better or even any different after the session apart from the fact that another person knew about my abuse and that is not what I wanted. I got the impression that his intention was for me to talk about it and then everything would be fine.' Hannah left the counselling room emotionally wrung out. 'I have since come to learn that the Bible doesn't say anything about having to talk about something to get over it; we don't necessarily need to dig up the past. Sometimes we may need to talk to someone for advice or counsel, but in my case it didn't necessarily have to be a psychiatrist,' she opines.

Hannah's next step forward was to take place five years later, at the age of twenty-two. Having attended her sister's wedding at Huddersfield Christian Fellowship, she decided to move to Huddersfield, become a member of the church and re-commit her life to God. While at one of the Sunday services she heard a church elder preaching about freedom from bondage to mental and emotional states. 'As he was speaking, I was thinking about my abuse but I thought I had been healed in that area,' she says. 'However, there were still some issues outstanding. One of them had become apparent when I started dating guys. My relationships with them were problematic because of how I felt about myself: very dirty, impure, very insecure, very unhappy about myself inside and just not a very nice person. Still like I had done something wrong.'

Songs of Freedom, a book detailing some of the work of the Freedom in Christ Ministries, talks about traumatic experiences from childhood being at the root of many people's problems and gives this explanation for Hannah's phenomenon:

'It's important to understand, however, that people are not in bondage to the traumatic event itself but to the lies they have come to believe as a result of the event. For example, those who have been sexually abused often come to believe as a result of their experiences that they are dirty. It's that feeling of dirtiness rather than the event itself that becomes the main problem.'[5]

Hearing the elder's teaching on the subject, Hannah joined the queue going forward for prayer 'because the Enemy was feeding me lies about myself. I knew he was telling me I was impure, dirty and worthless. I started to see that the reason I thought I would never amount to anything was because the Enemy had put those thoughts into my head. I realised I needed prayer to help me combat the lies and help me get an understanding of what God thought of me. I needed truth, which is God's Word, because I knew the truth would set me free. And it did. I moved on. So that was another leap. God had healed me from how I thought about myself.'

As it has been noted in *Songs of Freedom*, 'The truth is that no child of God is dirty any more – we have been washed completely clean by the blood of Jesus. Their healing comes when they are able to recognise the lie and start to believe the truth.'[6] God was clearly leading Hannah to recognise and be in a position to receive

---

5   Mitson, Eileen; Goss, Steve (2005) *Songs of Freedom Stories of Lives Transformed by the Deep Power of Christ,* Monarch Books p 153

6   Mitson, Eileen; Goss, Steve (2005) *Songs of Freedom Stories of Lives Transformed by the Deep Power of Christ,* Monarch Books p 153

help to counteract the obstacles that were hindering her from 'life in all its fullness'. Step by step He was guiding her into wholeness. As always, His timing was perfect as, soon after this intervention, Hannah met Michael Clarkson, the man who was to become her husband. But no sooner had this happened than another problem made itself known and Hannah was once again plunged into fear and confusion. 'I never wanted to get married,' she says. 'And as a Christian I knew that you only court with the intention of getting married. So all these thoughts were beginning to creep in again: "Do I want to let someone in that close? What if he does something to me? That's what men are like." Again it was lies from the Enemy but you still can't help having them when you've had something disturbing happen in your childhood. Michael and I started courting and I put these thoughts to one side but prayed about them.

'Before I met Michael, I had made myself accountable to Irene McKeegan (now Firth), a member of Huddersfield Christian Fellowship who had been a Christian for ten years. At the time I was struggling with my life as a Christian and realised that I needed help. I needed someone to be there to point me in the right direction when I was out of line. In keeping with the principles of accountability, I told her everything about myself and allowed her to advise and help me in my walk with the Lord. We became good friends. I shared with her from the outset about my sexual abuse but told her that I'd dealt with it and that I was fine, so at the time we didn't discuss the need for prayer. However, much further down the line and about the time I met Michael, I went round to see her and we watched a film, aspects of which brought back memories of my abuse. As the film progressed, Irene kept asking if I was OK with it and I was saying: "Yeah, I'm fine. I'm OK, I can watch it." I was trying to convince myself that there was nothing wrong when suddenly I broke down and cried. And I've never cried like that before. I was literally howling like an animal. Irene couldn't control me apart from putting her arms around me and cuddling me. And I was shaking. I was absolutely broken. I felt I had never been able to cry about it. I was never told it wasn't 'important' but I had the impression that there was nothing to talk about or discuss, whereas I was screaming inside: "Somebody help me out here." And this was a release.

'I felt I had never been allowed to share my feelings,' Hannah observes. 'It was all: "I've dealt with it. I'm fine. I'm strong. I can do this." But this particular evening I just went back to being this little girl all curled up in a ball, and I couldn't speak for ages. Irene just prayed that I would feel pure and whole, because I was still feeling impure. Although God had restored that in me, I needed to work at maintaining it because the Enemy knows our weaknesses and plays on them, and that was my vulnerable area.

'It was only later, when Irene asked if I had prayed for anything like this to happen, I remembered that only that morning, on my way to work, I had been praying that God would bring to the surface anything that needed to be dealt with in my life. I realised then that He had dealt with it immediately. I had had another breakthrough. You don't realise what prayer can do, do you?

'So there have been three points in my life where God has unmistakably worked in me. His Holy Spirit has been changing my heart and my mind, because it's not just your heart, it's your thought processes. It's changing our own perceptions of ourselves to God's perception of us. It's God who tells us who we are, that we're "fearfully and wonderfully made" (Psalm 139:14). So, we might have a past but He controls our future. I memorise scriptures to input into myself so that I can start believing what God says about me, that "for those who grieve ... [He] bestow[s] ... a crown of beauty instead of ashes" (Isaiah 61:3). Like Paul, "Forgetting what is behind and straining towards what is ahead, I press on towards the goal to win the prize for which God has called me heavenwards in Christ Jesus" (Philippians 3:13-14).

'We're a work in progress aren't we? Being "transformed into his likeness with ever-increasing glory" (2 Corinthians 3:18). And that's what I love about God. It would be easy for me to say: "Yeah, I want to be completely restored one hundred per cent right now," but God knows us better than we know ourselves. His timing is not our timing, but His timing is perfect. We wouldn't grow in our faith and dependence on Him if we had what we wanted when we wanted. I like that we're a 'work in progress'.

'When I look back now and think about how I was to my parents, I'm surprised they're still alive! The things I put them through, it's unbelievable. And they're still here, it's unconditional love. It's through them that I've been able to see God as a father figure, because of the love and affection in my life. The greatest thing of all is that through them I got to know Christ, my personal Saviour, my hope and strength. And it's through the grace of God that I am where I am today. I may have been in a terrible situation as a child but God has brought me closer to Him through it. I can say one hundred per cent that I don't regret, or I don't wish, or I don't resent the fact that I was sexually abused. There isn't any part of me that wishes it hadn't happened because I may not have had the relationship with God that I enjoy now. Because of what happened to me, because it affected my personality and was probably the reason why I went off the rails so badly, I came back to God. So it all connects. It brought me closer to God and through it I can help other people. And if I can help others then there's no way I would say that I wish it hadn't happened – if someone else can benefit from it.'

Hannah is now happily married to Michael. She is also part of the church worship team and on the day that she gave her heartfelt and emotive rendition of 'Great is Thy Faithfulness', there could have been no doubting, for those who knew of her struggles, that this timeless and beautiful hymn of God's love for us could have been written just for her.

Cathedral House, Huddersfield Christian Fellowship,
St Thomas' Road, Huddersfield HD1 3LG.
Tel: +44(0)1484 514088   www.huddersfieldchristianfellowship.com

Jon and Liz Harris and family.

Jacky Wisdom.

Sue Bond.

Colin Cooper
Pastor of Huddersfield
Christian Fellowship.

Jerry Lewis.

Searching for Healing
And Grace Elizabeth Harris

Growing up, half of me wanted to be glued to my comfort zone with my parents and the other to wander off in search of my own agenda. I had a great childhood and was very sporty and tennis mad. I grew up with my twin sister, but I did not know my older brother as he died at birth.

In September 1989 I attended a college in Wales for two years to study landscape design and attained a certificate in supervisory management. I made some good friends there but was very homesick. For some reason I found it difficult eating in front of other people and at college this developed into a non-eating routine. I also started drinking heavily and the combination of the two led to nervousness and anxiety followed by panic attacks. I learned to cope by hiding behind a mask of confidence, not letting anyone in or revealing what I thought was anything too weak or pathetic about myself. Eventually things got so bad that I tried to commit suicide but couldn't follow through with it. On returning home at the end of term I was able to confide in my parents who made arrangements for me to see a couple of psychologists, one at the local hospital and another privately. They diagnosed depression and prescribed antidepressants which either made my head spin or, conversely, made me feel listless and lethargic.

I had always had a fascination with spiritual matters and the New Age movement and now it gave me the buzz I was searching for as I tried to find a way to heal myself. Eventually it grew into an obsession. I attended classes for astrology and palmistry and developed like-minded friends through New Age magazines. I went to New Age conventions and met loads of people willing to share their experiences. Also I read books on crystal healing, chakra energies, pendulum power, tarot card reading, white witchcraft and even potion making. I have to say that my potions were revolting and made a mess of the kitchen! However, my depression continued in a far greater measure. Sometimes I would feel relaxed while at other times a sense of fear would creep over me.

Finally, after a hard slog, I completed my course, got a credit and worked as a landscape technician for a local nursery in Huddersfield. After that I moved back to Wales to work in a landscape architects' office in Ruthin and moved into a rather old cottage with a Spanish lady. She had similar interests to me spiritually, plus she was into ghost hunting! One afternoon we were digging in the back garden and found loads of old bones and skulls. After informing the police, we contacted our landlady who told us that the row of cottages had been built on top of a graveyard! The thought of dead people in the garden left me quite paranoid.

My Spanish friend had taken up going to church and I was asked if I wanted to go to an evangelical crusade in Rhyl. I remember standing at the top of the stairs pleading with her friends that I really didn't want to go and telling them all the reasons why, but it became apparent that they wouldn't leave without me. Reluctantly I went along with them and took my seat in the balcony. I remember seeing a lot of people being healed. One woman who had been crippled all her life walked for the first time and after she got out of her wheelchair I just burst into tears. I remember feeling a surge go through my body and felt as if somebody had literally lifted off my heavy depression. I don't remember any more of the service as I cried for most of it. It left me dumbfounded. I now know that what I experienced was God beginning to move in my life but at the time I wasn't the type of person to ask questions and so things went unexplained.

Eventually I moved away from Ruthin and got a job as a sales rep in Worksop selling rhododendrons to garden centres. The New Age scene, which I had abandoned in favour of attending a local Christian Fellowship following the crusade, once again started to hold an interest for me. My depression returned, only this time it was twice as bad. I went to see a lady who said she could heal my illness through talking with my inner guide. She waved lots of crystals and sweet smelling perfumes over my body which made me relax. She talked about communication with my guide and I had to imagine him taking me through the process. But on this occasion I couldn't see a thing and, after nearly an hour, had to confess that I'd fallen asleep and hadn't heard a word of it. I don't think she was happy at that point. Still, I tried it a few more times but couldn't get the hang of it. I also tried hypnotism, but that didn't work either.

While living in Worksop I eventually plucked up the courage to attend a church. I'd driven past quite a few and eventually got to know a Christian Fellowship through their bookshop. The people there were really nice. I explained my situation to them, about how I'd read New Age books in an effort to heal myself from depression. They explained to me that as Christians they believed it is only through the healing power of Jesus Christ that we can get fully healed, not through our own spiritual awareness.

With our prayerful perseverance, God is willing to heal us. I remembered that at the crusade, God had let me feel what it was like to be totally free from this bondage to depression. To me, this was great news and I began to seek God more by reading His Word and bombarding my new friends with countless questions. This changed my whole outlook on life.

On some weekends, I'd drive home to see my parents. I'd often go into the Huddersfield Christian Fellowship coffee shop to look at the CDs. The Fellowship was having a healing meeting one Sunday so I went along to the service. I remember feeling overwhelmed, as if I had come home. Something had fallen into place. I didn't get healed that night but I started to regularly attend the Sunday meetings.

My feelings of anxiety and sickness went on for another five years. But by going to church and reading His Word, my understanding of God's love and the sacrifice He made for me by sending His only Son to die in my place, grew deeper. It was during this time that I asked Jesus into my life by acknowledging that He died for me and that I can have a relationship with Him. Soon after this I was baptised in water. This is a command from God, symbolising the washing away of my sins, and of leaving my old life behind and entering into a new life. I was given this scripture to mark the event: 'So do not fear, for I am with you; do not be dismayed, for I am your God. I will strengthen you and help you; I will uphold you with my righteous right hand'. (Isaiah 41:10). A week later I was baptised in the Holy Spirit. This baptism equips us and gives us the power to overcome in Christ. 'For John baptised with water, but in a few days you will be baptised with the Holy Spirit' (Acts 1:5). Now I can talk to God any time, anywhere. But I think

God was asking me to totally trust in Him and not to rely on my own feelings.

At the church I met my husband, Jon, who had recently gone through a divorce and had left Leicestershire to live with his parents in Yorkshire. We got on very well but I still had problems with eating and this made it a little difficult when being asked out for meals. It was a difficult decision for me to get married as I didn't think it was fair to inflict my eating disorder on my future partner. But I loved Jon and knew that he was the right man for me. The night before the wedding I prayed and told God that I totally trusted Him to work things out. On my wedding day, my sickness disappeared I ate three meals: mine, a guest's and some of Jon's – and I have never again suffered with it.

My life as a Christian has, of course, had its ups and downs, but to totally trust and rely on God is well worth the struggle.

After four years of marriage, Jon and I decided that we wanted to start a family. In July 2003 I found out I was pregnant. My pregnancy went well, I had swelling on my feet and hands from eight months but this was normal. Our child's due date was 9 April 2004, Easter weekend. Jon's brother and sister-in-law and their family were staying with my in-laws nearby. My stepson was staying with us. We were all looking forward to celebrating Easter and the new baby.

On 6 April, five days before Easter, my blood pressure and protein levels became very high and I was sent to hospital to be monitored. By the next day my blood pressure had gone down and the baby was kicking well so I was sent home. On 9 April at 6 a.m. I felt the baby moving normally. At 9 a.m. we had a house call from our community midwife to check on my blood pressure, but the monitor could not detect the baby's heartbeat. We were rushed to hospital for a scan and further assessment. By 10a.m. it was confirmed that our baby had died.

We were devastated. We couldn't understand what had gone wrong. Jon rang both our sets of parents and I rang some of my friends from church. Incredibly, I do remember feeling very peaceful about it and was able to talk about the whole experience quite openly without breaking down at all, which is unusual for me as I am very sensitive. I know God was by my side at that time. The baby had still yet to be born. It is a mournful experience, knowing that you have to face a long labour with nothing to celebrate at the end of it. The doctors gave me a drug to bring on the birthing process. Two of my friends came to the hospital and prayed for us during the labour in a room at the end of the corridor.

The labour was OK although rather painful, and thankfully lasted just an hour. It was made more difficult by the fact that the baby was in the breech position. By the time the head appeared my contractions had stopped and I had to wait twenty minutes for further medication to take effect and bring on another set to complete the birthing process. Finally she was born. There was no crying, just silence. We didn't even know she was a girl until she was finally born. I'd always thought I was having a boy! We named her Grace Elizabeth. We held her little body and our family all took turns to hold her. We took lots of pictures. I was smiling throughout, totally relaxed. Jon and I spent that night in the hospital. I slept on and off but with a strange feeling of peace.

We held Grace's funeral at the church a week after Easter. We had so much wonderful support from family and friends throughout. Grace was buried in the same grave as my brother in a lovely little churchyard near Castle Hill, Huddersfield.

The hospital held an inquiry into Grace's death. They had an investigation of the medical records and interviews with the midwives and other staff. The reason for her death was given as 'placenta abrupta caused by a mild pre-eclampsia', which resulted in the placenta detaching itself from the wall of the womb, starving Grace of oxygen. She had been disconnected from the life-support system that should have kept her alive. We were told that, had I remained in hospital after the initial high blood pressure reading, there would have been little they could have done to save the baby after the placenta had become detached. There would have been less than a minute in which to get the baby out. Any longer would have resulted in her suffering severe brain damage with little chance of survival.

In a strange way, we look at the fact that she died as a blessing. Much as we would have wanted her with us, we believe she is in a much better place now. We hold firm to the belief that God has taken her to live with Him in Heaven and that one day, as Christians, we shall both see her again amid much rejoicing. We also believe that Grace died for a reason. If just one person comes to know God as a result of her death, whether by the word given at her funeral, this testimony, or our witness, then it was all worth it.

Throughout this whole ordeal, God was definitely by our side. He lifts us up when we need Him most, gives us the strength to go through such circumstances and only when we have the strength to carry on again on our own does He gently let us go. To persevere in such times is to trust God and be reassured that He is always by our side, no matter what we go through.

****

When Liz gave her testimony, she was looking forward to the birth of their second child. She wrote: 'With only three weeks of the pregnancy left, I am confident that this time it will be a joyous occasion. And I totally put my faith and trust in Jesus Christ.' Liz's confidence was well placed and she gave birth to a healthy baby son, Samuel James Harris on 21 September 2005. Two and a half years later, on 8t April 2008, Anna Grace Harris was born.

Jon and Liz have been able to use their experience with Grace to help other couples in similar situations.

JACKY WISDOM

We are hard pressed on every side, but not crushed;
perplexed, but not in despair; persecuted, but not
abandoned, struck down, but not destroyed.
(2 Corinthians 4:8-9)

We all go through difficulties in life and sometimes there are things which happen that we think we will never be able to get through. We all have different approaches and coping mechanisms which we draw on through these hard times. I would like to share with you how I have got through my life circumstances.

Fifteen years ago, my husband, Roger, was unemployed. We had not been married very long, had bought our first little house and had a small baby with another on the way. This was not a situation we had expected and, as such, had made no contingency plans. The weeks moved into months, and, for nearly two years, this situation continued. My husband had a file full of rejection letters and we wondered when something would come along that would enable him to support the family. I learned to budget, to be frugal, and discovered how to conjure up a meal with virtually nothing! It certainly was not the way we had planned our early married life. However, at those times when despair may have come, when I was juggling bills to pay and walking miles with pushchair in tow to find the cheapest shopping, I knew I was not alone. We learned humility as we looked to God to be our provider, rather than at our own ability to provide, and we learned to give to others from the little we had, rather than waiting for others to give to us in our time of need. It did not matter how little we had, we never went without!

'We are hard pressed on every side, but not crushed'

Two years later, now with three children, I awoke in the middle of the night to hear a piercing scream. I recognised it as that of our eldest daughter. I realised very quickly that something dreadful was wrong and, upon opening the girls' bedroom door, was unable to enter due to thick, acrid smoke pouring out of the room. Roger sent me to get our son, Felix, from the adjoining bedroom and remove him to a place of safety, while he rescued Poppy and Blossom from the burning room. He could not breathe as he entered the bedroom, nor could he see anything. When he reached Blossom's bed, he realised that she had snuggled right under the covers. This was most unusual as we usually had to pull her down into the bed to ensure she remained covered. She was only eighteen months old at the time. When he got to Poppy's bed, he could hear her screams but could not see her; he could just about make out there were flames and thought she was on fire. As he batted the flames down, he burned his hand. It was then that he realised she was sitting on the corner of her bed, the flames in front of her. The fire brigade were called and proceeded to get things under control. They said they were amazed that our children had stayed in bed, as often in these situations little ones become frightened and try to hide elsewhere in order to get away from the fire.

At the hospital we were all checked over. The doctors could not believe the blood gas results, they were perfectly normal! No carbon monoxide or other toxic chemicals normally associated with smoke inhalation were detected. Poppy had only suffered some small burns. The most serious problem was the burn Roger had sustained to his hand. We were told that he could require skin grafting as a result but in the event it healed quickly and naturally, without the need for surgical intervention. I know we were all protected from danger that night. Had I not awoken when I did, the path from our attic bedroom to the children's rooms would have been blocked and we would have been overcome with smoke. Our house was devastated with smoke damage, we lost most of our possessions. But the most precious of all, our lives, were saved.

'Perplexed, but not in despair'

Two-and-a-half years later, baby number four, Amelia, arrived. She was beautiful, the other children doted on her. At eight weeks of age, she became unwell. What initially appeared to be symptoms of an infection very quickly led to an emergency admission to the Paediatric Oncology Unit at a hospital in Leeds. We knew this was more than an infection and, as a qualified nurse myself, I knew this was serious. Within hours Amelia was diagnosed with an extremely rare condition: familial erythrophagocytic lymphohistiocytosis. This meant that the cells which usually 'clean up' the blood were proliferating uncontrollably and were infiltrating all of her major organs, preventing them from functioning properly. This was one seriously ill girl. Talks of chemotherapy, steroids, intrathecal therapy (involving the tissue membranes lining the brain and spinal cord) and operations all became a reality rather than the textbook lessons I had learned in nursing school.

It is impossible to try and explain what it is like for a mother to sit and watch her young daughter struggle to maintain life. The treatments were so harsh and gave rise to so many horrendous side effects that for most of the time a nurse had to be with her constantly. I telephoned the 'prayer chain' at church, where members pray for people in need. As the days turned into months, I wrote a prayer diary and sent it to people we knew, in order for them to pray for Amelia and the family. As each new treatment brought its own problems, we prayed against each side effect affecting Amelia. At home, a team of friends provided meals, collected the children from school and undertook the housework (wow!) which enabled us to concentrate on our children. I met another mother of a little girl who had the same condition as Amelia. She understood very little of the English language but we managed to communicate in small ways as our little girls received their treatment. At eight months of age, Amelia underwent a bone marrow transplant, with our son being the donor (the best match you can have is a sibling donor). This is when Amelia's little friend died, her body unable to cope any longer with the effects of the disease and its treatment. The stark reality was that children with this condition have a very poor prognosis.

While Amelia was recovering, my father died, my mother-in-law died, and I was proceeding with an industrial tribunal as my employment had been unfairly terminated at the onset of Amelia's illness. Life was tough. Amelia continued to make progress and was finally allowed home. At twenty-one months of age she was finally able to have all her tubes removed and our lives began to return to normal.

'Persecuted, but not abandoned'

Three months later our fifth child was born, the smallest of the children and looking like a little doll. As I nursed her in the small hours, I knew I had to cherish her. Five weeks later, she was sent as an emergency admission to the Paediatric Intensive Care Unit of the same hospital Amelia had been admitted to before. Madeline had the same condition as Amelia. However, this time I knew it was different. Some may call it a mother's instinct; only a mother can explain this. As I watched the consultants mumble together and saw the monitor figures, I knew what was happening. As the 'prayer chain' prayed for healing for Madeline, I knew it was to be a different healing to that of Amelia's. I held her in my arms as the machinery was turned off, and then bathed her as the last loving act a mother could perform for her child.

'Struck down, but not destroyed'

Six years later, we returned from a holiday of a lifetime in Florida to discover the babbling brook which trickled through our garden had become a river which had re-routed through our home! The bottom floor of our house was covered in stinking mud sludge with water marks over three feet up the walls as the waters had risen. For the next eight months we bedded down in friends' houses, hotels and rented accommodation until we were able to move back into our home.

These things are not written to create pity about our circumstances, or pride about the way we have overcome our situations. We are not special people who are strong and courageous, nor do we take the credit for being able to manage in these difficult circumstances – after all, we have cried and we have grieved as any other person would have done. Rather, we are ordinary people who have found something very special in life. We have found a relationship with God. In the normal way of things, we could not have coped easily with any one of these life events. But one thing that we know is that when our strength was becoming weak, God gave us strength; when our despair began to rise, God gave us hope; when we felt alone, God was our companion; and when love faded, God comforted us with His love.

Commit your way to the Lord;
trust in him and he will do this:
He will make your righteousness shine like the dawn,
the justice of your cause like the noonday sun.
(Psalm 37:5-6)

BRIAN & CHRISTINE NICHOLS

I will strengthen you and help you (Isaiah 41:10)

Why? Why is it that life can sometimes be so hard? Why is it that sometimes we find ourselves in situations so unendurable that simply getting through another day is an unadulterated victory, the conquering of our own personal Everest? The simple answer is, sometimes there is no answer. But maybe that's because we're asking the wrong question. Instead of 'why?' maybe we should be asking 'who?' Who will point us in the right direction? Who will help us in our desperate predicament? Brian and Christine learned the truth of this when each faced their own overwhelming dilemmas ...

It was to mark Queen Elizabeth II's coronation on 2 June 1953 that an eight-year old Christine, along with the other children in her school, received a copy of the Bible. Born just after the Second World War into a family headed by a loving mother but also a heavy-drinking, abusive father, she had to go without most of the things that other children perhaps took for granted. Never can she remember having so much as a toy. So when she was presented with this souvenir of the royal occasion, she valued it and kept it as her most treasured possession.

Some years later, when each of her three elder brothers had fled the nest, Christine was left alone without her siblings to cope with an ever-worsening situation at home. Escaping the charged and acrimonious atmosphere downstairs she would head to the relative peace of her bedroom and the comfort of her precious gift, which she was now old enough to read and appreciate. 'I can still remember feeling a real warmth and thinking: "Oh, I wish that it was true"," she says. 'I believed in God, but I didn't really understand. But that's how I think that God first came into my life.'

At fifteen, Christine left school to work as a mender. 'It was one of the best-paid jobs in the mill at that time and I couldn't wait to have some money of my own. I wanted to get away from home as soon as I possibly could,' she remembers. 'And then I met my first boyfriend at sixteen and married him at nineteen. By the age of twenty-two I had two sons.'

Although the marriage wasn't perfect, Christine was content with life. The first intimation, however, that anything was seriously wrong came during the Christmas of 1982. 'We had been married seventeen years by this time and I found out that my husband and my best friend were having an affair and she was expecting his baby,' she says. 'My friend later told me that as soon as she saw my husband, she knew she was going to get him. I was devastated. I couldn't believe that I had been deceived and betrayed by the two people who meant so much to me. My world just seemed to stop. I remember looking out of the window and not seeing or feeling anything. I just stood there for four days. I didn't know how to cope.'

Beyond the numbing shock, however, her main concern was for the future of their two young sons. Hard workers both and performing well at school, university was a real possibility. At that time, only the highest achievers, the top two per cent in the country, gained access to these highly-regarded and sought-after institutions. She considered their prospects now, worried that should her husband leave their chances of going on to higher education might be affected. 'He was a good father and I didn't want their lives plagued by it all. So I just carried on trying to keep things normal and didn't tell anyone,' she states simply. 'My husband talked about leaving, but he never did. He stayed but, unbeknown to me, didn't end the affair.'

Christine struggled on, isolated in her private pain. 'I don't know how I got through that time,' she reflects. 'I didn't tell a soul and keeping something like that to yourself is quite hard. But out of the blue, eighteen months later as I was going through a supermarket checkout, an acquaintance who I didn't see often asked if I'd like to come to church that Sunday. She said that an evangelist would be coming and they had been asked to invite people along. Although I didn't go to church, she was so nice to me that I decided to go.'

And so it was through a simple invitation that Christine came to hear the healing words that would transform her life. 'I went to church that night and when the evangelist spoke, it was just like he was speaking only to me,' she says. He said: "No matter what has happened in your life, God loves you. There might be something in your life that you can't tell anyone about. You might feel you can't trust anyone and think nobody cares about you, nobody loves you. But I'm here to tell you that Jesus loves you and He knows what you're going through. He sees all your pain and suffering and He wants to help you. He wants to be in your life." I couldn't believe what I was hearing. Nobody knew how I felt but he was talking about what was happening to me. His message really affected me and I know that God spoke to me that night through this man. I listened intently to what he said and that night, I knelt by my bed and asked for forgiveness for anything I had done wrong (although I didn't think that I *had* done anything wrong) and asked Jesus to come into my life. Then I just said: "Will You help me?" God met me where I was and gave me an overwhelming desire to read the Bible and I just wanted to be in church. I started going and couldn't get enough of it.

'Now that I knew God, I thought that everything would be OK and my marriage would be restored. I didn't understand then that it's not all about getting what you want and things actually got worse for me. I found out that my former friend had had another baby and I knew straight away that it was my husband's. Still I told no-one. But God gave me strength when I had none of my own. He had spoken to me through a Bible verse when I first asked Him into my life:

So do not fear, for I am with you;
do not be dismayed, for I am your God.
I will strengthen you and help you;
I will uphold you with my righteous right hand.
(Isaiah 41:10)

'That meant so much to me and I knew then that whatever happened, God would never let me down. It's my all-time favourite verse.

'Time went by and eighteen months later I was out shopping when I saw my former friend walking towards me pushing a pram, the older child walking by her side. She was also heavily pregnant. She saw me and carried on coming. At that moment I just wanted to hit her but I cried out an emergency prayer to God: "Lord, You have got to help me. What am I going to do?" I felt like crying, but at she came towards me, my attitude changed completely. I invited her to come with me for a coffee and God gave me the strength to listen and talk to her for three hours; it was really strange because I was able to talk to her normally. When I saw her that day, I would say it was one of the hardest times in my life. It was so hard, my feelings were all over the place. But God had given me His grace just when I needed it. Without Him in my life, it would have been impossible for me to behave the way I did.'

Christine's sons did go on to university and, following their graduations, left home. Christine stayed with her husband but by the time her marriage was in its twenty-seventh year, she had 'lived with no love for ten years' and in the final year the stress had caused her to lose weight dramatically. Moreover, her husband had decided on a course of action which would have made her, already bleak, future intolerable. To protect those involved, Christine does not feel able to go into the details. 'However, I gave him an ultimatum,' Christine says. 'I said if he chose to go ahead with his plan, I would tell our sons what had been going on all these years. I pleaded with him to change his mind, but he wouldn't. I was crying about this when one of my sons called unexpectedly. He thought I was ill when he saw me and I told him the truth about everything. He couldn't believe what had been happening as he had known nothing about it and he told my husband to leave. It was an unbelievable shock for both my sons and the whole family was devastated. However, those ten years had been like a bereavement for me and when he left I only felt relief. When my other son arrived and found out about the awful situation, he asked me how I could be so strong. I told him that God was giving me the strength I needed, and it was so true. I said I wanted things to be OK between them and their dad as he had been a good father to them. There had been so many bad times, so many wild times, and for me to be so sure that I wanted them to continue to have a relationship could only have been due to God working in me.

'He sustained and provided for me in other ways, too. One issue with me was forgiveness. I had struggled with this for many years and didn't know if I could forgive my husband and former friend. They haven't even said they were sorry! I couldn't cope with it all and I couldn't forgive. But then I thought, hadn't God forgiven me? How could I then not forgive? Once I realised this, God helped me to do what would have been impossible in my own strength and I can say now, without question, that I have forgiven them and have no bitterness in my heart at all. There is no malice, no anger, or anything and that is an absolute testimony of what God can do.

'Another thing was that I hadn't had any love shown to me by my husband and I just wanted to be loved. I'm quite a loving person and I remember praying a lot to God about this, saying that I just wanted to be loved for me. Then a year later, I met Brian through mutual friends and he just bowled me over.'

Here, Brian takes up the story: 'We got on well together and the first thing she told me was that she was a Christian. My former wife was also a Christian and I blamed her beliefs for driving a wedge between us so I was against the whole thing. But it somehow didn't put me off Christine. I took her for a meal and we went for a walk holding hands and everything was special. On our way back to the car, I stopped and bought her some flowers and she cried because she said no-one had ever bought her flowers before. We started going out together and used to stay up talking until two in the morning. We had so much to talk about. I asked her if I could go to church with her and started going every week.

As a result of this, and our growing relationship, I too gave my life to God and became a Christian.'

Brian and Christine married and life settled into a routine, working during the week and socialising at pubs and clubs in the evenings and at weekends. It was this latter aspect of their life together that highlighted an issue that was becoming progressively more disturbing for them both. 'I used to drink before we went out,' he says. 'And I started to drink heavily, sometimes having a shot of vodka at the bar while I was ordering. This often caused arguments and I started being verbally abusive.' The pattern had been set in motion years before he knew Christine, when he had spent many hours drinking in pubs with friends, often catching only a couple of hours sleep before heading off to work. Now he was drinking frequently at home, often in secret, and it wasn't until he realised that he was consuming more and more alcohol to feel any effect at all that alarm bells began to ring.

'Although I was a Christian, I wasn't living a Christian life,' he confesses. 'I was in trouble but I didn't want to admit it to myself. Christine kept telling me that I had a problem with drink but I would push all thoughts about it away, convinced that I could handle it. Things started to get much worse as the alcohol took its toll. Although I didn't drink in the mornings (and therefore thought I wasn't an alcoholic), as soon as I got home from work I would start drinking and carry on all night. I depended on it. I didn't want to eat, just drink. It replaced my food and sometimes when I did eat, I was sick.'

Looking back, Brian now concedes that the years of heavy drinking had culminated in his loss of control over, and dependence upon, alcohol. At the time he knew he had a serious problem. 'I kept coming to church but deep inside I felt so ashamed knowing I was an alcoholic,' he says. 'I went to a few places looking for help, but nothing really helped me. Eventually Christine and I went to see one of our church elders, Jerry Lewis, and his wife, Rosa. I remember feeling very frightened of what they might think of me but they didn't judge me. They just showed me love and encouragement. They said I was in a trap that I couldn't get out of myself and I needed to depend on Jesus to help me by the power of His Holy Spirit. I kept on going to church but I knew I wasn't giving my problem to God. I knew I would have another drink. Drink was always on my mind.'

Meanwhile, at home, the situation was becoming intolerable. 'Alcohol is very powerful. It doesn't just affect you, it affects your whole family and friends as well. It robs you of everything,' Brian admits and adds with unflinching honesty: 'My personality totally changed and I said some awful things and was aggressive. I just didn't care about hurting the people around me. I was so selfish that I had to have my drink before anything else. It got so bad that Christine had to go to a friend's house until I had fallen into a drunken stupor. The police had to be called on a number of occasions, usually because I was outside banging on the windows and doors, shouting abuse because Christine was too scared to let me in. I never realised what she was going through and she ended up being off work for ten weeks with the stress of it all. She was emotionally exhausted.

'Eventually she told me that she couldn't carry on with the way things were any more and that I had to leave. She didn't want us to split up but she did want to bring me to my senses. I ended up moving into a flat and at first all I could think was that I could do what I wanted and drink what I wanted. But the flat was awful and it wasn't long before I felt really alone and desperate. I remembered Jerry's words, that I couldn't fight the problem on my own. I started praying and reading the Bible. During all this time I was still attending church. I'd meet up with Christine beforehand and we'd go in together so no one knew that we were living apart. One Sunday I felt so bad that I fell to my knees during the worship. That day, Jerry was preaching and his message centred on surrendering everything to God. I felt the Holy Spirit convicting me of my sin and I knew this time it was different. I had to give it all to God. As soon as I made my decision I felt a release. It was like a heavy weight had been lifted off my shoulders and I knew that God had healed me. And when I say healed, I mean that He healed everything, my body and my mind, just like that. I stopped drinking and didn't suffer from any withdrawal symptoms, no shakes or anything. Alcoholics who have been sober for many years struggle because they still want to drink, but know that they can't because of the consequences. But since that Sunday, over five years ago now, I haven't had a drink or any desire to drink.

'Shortly after my healing I had to have a series of medical tests, including a liver test because of my history of drinking, and they all came back normal. After all the years of alcohol abuse, my liver was perfect! And for that I give all the glory to God. I sometimes sit at home and think: "Wow! I'm healed. God healed me! What a blessing." I can honestly say that without God in my life I don't know where I'd be today. I was looking for help everywhere with my addiction and yet the help was here with me all the time.'

Brian and Christine's marriage was saved and they are now firmly back together. They found the answer to both their problems was Jesus.

*And the prayer offered in faith will make
the sick person well.* (James 5:15)

For several months towards the end of 2005 I was in a lot of pain in my lower back and felt generally unwell. My doctor arranged several tests including some blood tests and, having obtained the results, referred me to a kidney specialist. At the appointment, the specialist arranged for me to have a scan and I was told to return in two weeks' time for the results. The church prayer team prayed for me. My church elders also prayed with me and I was anointed with oil, after which my pain just went.

When I went back for the results, the scan showed a cyst on one kidney and a large kidney stone on the other. There was also a shadow in my left renal area. I was asked to return for another scan using contrast dye in three days' time to further investigate the cyst and kidney stone and to explore the shadow.

On the way home my husband and I called to see Jerry and Rosa Lewis, one of the church elders and his wife. While we were there I received a call on my mobile asking me to return to the hospital the following morning for the tests. The next day, the test that should have taken about an hour lasted almost three hours. I had the scan with contrast dye and an X-ray but nothing abnormal was detected. So I then had to undergo a CT (computed tomography) cross-sectional scan to show the area in more detail.

A few days later I went back to see the specialist for the results. He was clearly dumbfounded. Displaying both sets of scans, he showed me how in the first set the cyst, kidney stone and shadow were all clearly visible. In the second scan they had all disappeared! He said that he couldn't understand it and that the kidney stone alone was so large that it couldn't possibly have been passed out of my body in the normal way. It would have had to be shattered by a laser. I knew what had happened, though. Praise God, I had been healed.

God Won My Heart

A slight, dapper figure, Jerry arrived in Huddersfield in 1999 from South Africa. As one of Huddersfield Christian Fellowship's church elders, he radiates gentleness and compassion, qualities which are reflected in the tone of his sermons and shared by his supportive and caring wife, Rosa. A strong woman in her own right, she is so spiritually attuned to her Father in Heaven and through Him, the needs of others, that even as she was undergoing debilitating treatment for a major illness, she was able to accurately perceive during the course of a general conversation that I was in the throes of a very real dilemma. Her comforting words and prayers of assurance enabled me to finally put the situation to rest, knowing that God was in control and that what I feared most would not happen. And indeed two years on from our conversation, it still hasn't.

God's command to 'love your neighbour as yourself' (Leviticus 19:18) is certainly true of Jerry and Rosa. Together, they make people feel special. It's not a 'talent' they've had to work on, it's simply their way of being; in the things they do and say and the genuine affection they have for everyone they come into contact with. One congregant has spoken of Jerry lavishing his love on us. But such a trait often has its roots in personal suffering, and Jerry is no exception.

'I was born in Zambia in 1959 and grew up in a very non-Christian family,' Jerry begins. 'My parents didn't teach me anything about God. They drank heavily, especially at weekends, and there was always lots of fighting so my home life was very chaotic. The relationship between myself and my parents wasn't good.'

Jerry's father worked as an underground miner at the wealthy Anglo-American owned copper mines and could therefore ensure that his son received a first-rate, exclusive education. Despatched to a very smart, religious boarding school in Rhodesia (now Zimbabwe) governed by the Church, he discovered that a rigorous devotional routine and strict discipline were high on the agenda. 'The school gave me my first awareness of God. I knew nothing of God at all until then,' Jerry reiterates. 'But it had nothing to do with having a relationship with God. It was church twice a day, once in the morning before class and then in the evening after supper. At the weekends these services were very protracted and all the kids had to stand almost the whole way through them. Very often you'd hear a thud and we all knew that sound well. It was a kid fainting. It happened all the time. Then there were the punishments. One of the priests there was especially strict. He would come down on us severely if we did anything wrong or spoke out of turn. Quite apart from hitting us, his favourite form of discipline was making us carry boxes of Bibles on our heads from the classroom, down to the playing fields and back again. While the other kids were playing, you'd be sweating carrying these huge boxes and they were really heavy. Sometimes you could only take a few steps uphill before you had to put the box down and get your breath back. And that was my introduction to God. I saw this priest as His representative and was shocked and horrified at the whole concept of God as an old man up in heaven with a long grey beard beating people.'

It was not a good start. Things, however, were about to get a lot worse. Alerted by the school, Jerry's parents flew their twelve-year-old son to a children's hospital in Johannesburg to investigate a swollen lump in his neck which was not responding to treatment. Exhaustive tests revealed Hodgkin's disease, an uncommon form of cancer normally found in adults. 'The hospital had not come across this in a child before,' Jerry explains. 'I don't think they could quite believe it. For a couple of days they had specialist teams coming to prod and poke to see what it was. But the tests did prove positive. The lump was removed and this was followed by abdominal surgery to investigate the spread of the cancer, after which my spleen was removed. It was a time of real turmoil for me. I'd been wrenched out of my school environment and now this was happening to me.

'The doctors were very concerned and told my parents that the prognosis was not good at all. Although they didn't hold out much hope for me, they said that they would be prepared to continue my treatment with radium therapy which would take place over the next few months. By this time my father had to return to work in Zambia and my mother flew home with him so I was left alone in the hospital; no parents, no relatives and no-one there I knew. And then the treatment started. Every day the ambulance picked me up from the children's hospital and transported me to the main hospital in the city which had the resources to carry out my treatment. That was the worst time of all for me because they would irradiate my whole body and I would feel such nausea. Afterwards the trip back was just terrible and when I arrived back at the children's hospital, I would run for the toilets and vomit. This would happen two, three, four times a night, every night. It was so humiliating because it was happening during visiting hours and I could feel everyone looking at me. I had no support and it was a really dark time for me.'

Concerned about his missed schooling, the educational authorities advised that he be sent to a specialist home and boarding school for young people with physical disabilities. It was felt that this would be the best place to cater for both his scholastic and medical needs as he still required daily treatment. 'But it was a disastrous decision,' Jerry asserts. 'I was very ill and had lost a lot of weight but I had my hands, my fingers, my feet, my toes. All the other residents there either had something missing or something physically wrong with them and I was resented because I had all my limbs. But I remember this one lady, she must have been in her early twenties and she was probably one of the worst cases in the home. She didn't have any legs or arms, she just had hands at the ends of her shoulders on each side; it was a terrible sight to see. But she had the sweetest, most beautiful spirit, I still remember her to this day. She would talk about God and she just had such love in her heart. She warmed towards me and was so encouraging. Sadly she died while I was there. She contracted pneumonia and couldn't fend it off. I had a lot of anger directed towards me from a lot of the people there but the way she had been made a huge impact on me in relation to my understanding of God.

'After two months at the home I was sent back to the hospital as it wasn't working out. But God is faithful, He never gives up! I began to receive letters from some of the kids in the boarding school and these kids had a relationship with the Lord. A real one. They had all got together and began to pray for me and they wrote that they were trusting God to do a great work in me. Then I began to get letters from other schools. I think the word just began to spread and it was such a remarkable thing to get letters from kids that I didn't even know. They were treating it as a prayer project and it was a divine thing, God almost rallied prayer. He can do things on His own but sometimes He wants us to work with Him (For we are God's fellow-workers', 1 Corinthians 3:9).

'But the turning point came one day when I was feeling absolutely rotten; I later learned that it was a real touch and go situation. I was lying in my hospital bed when I felt somebody touching my arm. Opening my eyes, I saw a guy standing there. He just smiled at me and said: "Can I pray for you?" And all kinds of feelings welled up in my heart. I'd been receiving letters which were encouraging but I still wasn't convinced about this God. There was still a lot of hatred and confusion. But when I looked at him … I can't describe the look on his face but he was just so calm that I said: "Yes, you can pray," and I remember feeling very frightened because I kept remembering the priest at boarding school. This man then laid hands on me (a biblical principle when praying for a particular need), prayed a short prayer and left. But from that point on there was a dramatic turnaround. The results of my blood tests were so much better that it wasn't long before I was sent home to recuperate. I had to have regular check-ups: monthly, then twice a year, then annually until eventually I was given the all clear. I was free of cancer. I'm forty-seven years old now, it was a long time ago. A remarkable time of God intervening through prayer.'

After having recovered sufficiently to go back to boarding school, Jerry pushed all thoughts of God to the back of his mind. 'I knew deep down that God had touched me and healed me, but I didn't want to give Him my life,' he acknowledges. 'The terrible situation at home made me turn against Him and I would often ask: "God, why did you allow this to happen?" I'd shout and swear at Him to leave me alone. I ended up rebelling and by the age of sixteen I was drinking heavily. At boarding school my friends and I would pay the kitchen chefs to smuggle drink in for us. We'd go to weddings and get completely blasted under the table. I hated what I was doing but didn't know why I was doing it. I'd remember the early years as a kid in my home and glasses getting thrown around and all the swearing and carrying on, and yet I was doing the same thing and couldn't stop it. I knew I was going downhill, but as much as I hated what the alcohol was doing, I just seemed to go for it.

'But then something happened. I'd left school by this time and one of my good friends had joined the Army. He'd come back on leave and I wanted us to go out drinking but he told me that he didn't do that any more. His behaviour had totally changed. "I've given my life to Jesus," he said. I couldn't believe it. "What? Are you mad?" I asked him. "After everything we've been through at boarding school?" Because we'd been together through those years and he'd been as anti-Christian as me'. Deciding that his friend had obviously joined some kind of religious sect, Jerry set about devising a plan to rescue him from the clutches of this evil cult. 'But he just spoke to me,' Jerry says. 'He impressed upon me that God wasn't like the old priest from boarding school. He kept telling me that God loved me and I just found myself immersed in His love.'

Going to his first evangelical church service, Jerry still felt unsure and not a little apprehensive. 'I walked through the front doors and I was so nervous because I could see these people singing and clapping,' he remembers. 'I just kept watching the back doors to see if we were going to be locked in. If they just move towards those doors, I thought, I'm running out. But as I stood there and looked around and watched those people lifting their hands and worshipping the Lord, I began to weep because I could see there was something real there. And all of that stuff over the years – the priests punishing us, the resentment and anger about what had happened in my life – it all came to the surface. At that point I knew that my conception of God as this old man in Heaven with a long beard hurting me and putting sickness on me had been wrong all along. I realised that He was a loving God who wanted a relationship with me. In the end, God won my heart. And from that time on, I've never been the same again.'

And all of us who know him have nothing but the deepest respect for the sweet-natured, genuinely humble and understanding man he has become.

****

Sadly, Jerry is no longer with us. Although it is painful for those left behind, Jerry stepped over the threshold into the loving arms of his Maker on January 11 2008, just three months after being diagnosed with metastatic bowel cancer. He was incredibly peaceful with leaving this world because he knew that his destiny was eternity. He believed the same was possible for every life he touched.

My Healing from Cancer

My name is Margaret Cutler. I am in my sixties and I have been a Christian for over forty years. During that time I have seen God act miraculously many times in my life and have known His guidance and influence in many ways. However, there is one particular situation in my life that I would like to tell you about – how God healed me of cancer.

In August 1999, at the age of fifty-two, I developed a severe pain in my left lower abdomen, which was diagnosed as an ovarian cyst and led to me having a semi-emergency hysterectomy (removal of the uterus) and oophorectomy (removal of the ovaries). It is unusual for ovarian cysts to make themselves known in this way, but in my case the cyst had got trapped in my pelvis and the pressure had caused the pain. I believe that this was the first of God's many interventions.

After the operation, the laboratory report came back – the 'cyst' was a cancerous tumour, of a particularly malignant type. I had ovarian cancer. Ovarian cancer is known as the silent killer, as it often causes no symptoms until it is advanced and incurable. The fact that the cyst got trapped and was removed early, before the cancer had had time to spread, was to me, a blessing from God.

Because of the malignant nature of the tumour and other technical issues, it was recommended that I had a course of chemotherapy. Norman, my husband, and I had prayerfully decided that we would follow the doctor's suggestions, unless we felt very clearly that God was directing us otherwise, so I had the chemotherapy. It was given as six doses at three-weekly intervals from September 1999 to January 2000. Not quite how I had envisaged celebrating the Millennium! During all this I went through many emotions – disbelief, fear, acceptance, doubt, hope – you name it, I probably experienced it. Through it all I knew God was in control, and as I became weaker and more tired because of the chemotherapy, I had a greater sense of God's love and the fact that He never allows us to face more than we can cope with. I was also helped greatly by the love and care shown to me by friends at church. I had so many letters, cards, phone calls, visits, help – it was wonderful to feel so cared for.

In January 2000, I was told that there was no evidence of disease. I recovered from the effects of the chemotherapy (my hair grew back!) and I returned to work in April 2000, feeling well and rejoicing that I had come through a difficult time, supported by God's love.

I thought it was all over – but I had only reached the end of part one. Part two was to follow and it would be much more testing. Although I had cancer, up to this point everything had been positive – the message was: 'We've caught it early; there is no sign of any spread; it should be curable'. I should survive, or, at least, the statistics said I had an eighty to eighty-five per cent chance of doing so.

About the end of April 2000, I started to feel some pain in my abdomen. It came and went, moved around from place to place and I became concerned. I had an appointment at the hospital in Leeds where I had had all my chemotherapy where an examination showed nothing. The doctor decided I should have a CT scan (a specialised form of X-ray examination) to check all was well. I had the scan at the beginning of July and returned to clinic on 24 July, expecting to be told all was well. Instead, I was told that the cancer had returned only months after the end of chemotherapy, that all the indications were that it was very aggressive, and that my life expectancy was now six months to two years, depending on how well things went. I felt as if I had dropped into a very deep, dark hole. It was unexpected; it was the opposite of what I thought God was doing in my life.

Then things started to happen! When I got home and told my husband and my mother (who was on holiday with us at the time), Norman immediately phoned the church prayer team for support. Colin Cooper, our pastor, phoned and asked if we would like to come over to the church next day, so they could pray for us. The next day, a group, including elders, a visiting pastor from Kenya, and some of the prayer team met with us and we prayed. The atmosphere in that room was electric. There was a supernatural presence – the power of God was there. The despair and darkness which had ensnared me the previous day lifted and I never felt it again. Please understand that did not mean that I was never down, never felt anxious, never had black moments again. But it was a quality of despair which left and never returned.

My treatment had yet to be decided and I had to await the outcome of several medical discussions before I knew what would be suggested. By August I knew. They felt that because the cancer had reoccurred in only one place, that it was worth attempting surgery to remove it, followed by radiotherapy to destroy any remaining disease. I saw the surgeon and he explained very clearly that there were considerable risks. He felt it was a very difficult operation, with a possible risk of damaging blood or nerve supply to bladder and bowels, and that it was possible that he might be unable to remove all of the tumour, or would find that it had spread, bearing in mind how rapidly it had grown up until now. However, overall he thought it was worth attempting the removal if I were willing to accept the risks, which I was.

Surgery was scheduled for the end of August. In the intervening time, many things happened that showed me God was in control of the situation, and was caring for me. I will give details of two things to show how God was working. The first was like a three-part jigsaw, with three individual small incidents coming together to form a complete picture. I was praying with a friend and she said she felt that I had to be like a toddler holding on to her parent; they do so in utter trust and confidence. That was how I was to hold on to God. This immediately sparked a memory for me. When I was twenty-one and waiting for my degree results, God spoke clearly to me through a preacher at church. The words were part of a story he was telling, but for me they seemed to be written in letters of fire on the church wall! They were: 'I've been with you this far, I will not leave you now.' In the intervening thirty plus years, I know that this has been true, and it was a reminder and a confirmation that I could really trust God – like a toddler. The third piece of the jigsaw came on a card from an old friend, who had just heard about what was happening. She had written on the bottom of the card Isaiah 46 verse 4, which, along with the end of verse 3, confirmed the other two pieces. It says: 'You whom I have upheld since you were conceived, and have carried since your birth. Even to your old age and grey hairs I am he, I am he who will sustain you. I have made you and I will carry you; I will sustain you and I will rescue you.'

The second thing was a dream I had when I was in hospital awaiting the surgery. I dreamt I was being chased by a large letter C that had sharp teeth and was trying to devour me, an obvious analogy to the cancer. I was backed into a corner with no escape, when suddenly all the teeth fell out and the C collapsed, deflated. I believe that this was God saying that He had disarmed the cancer and that it would not devour me.

I had the surgery on 31 August 2000. I remember little of the day, except that I faced it with an amazing sense of peace, knowing all would be well because it was in God's hands. When I saw the surgeon after the operation, all he could say was that it was amazing, one of the easiest operations he had ever done. The tumour just popped out into his hands and there was no sign of any cancer anywhere else. The operation had taken half the time he had expected and there were absolutely no complications to worry about! This, from one of the most experienced gynaecological cancer surgeons in the country! I knew God had answered our prayers, despite the gloomy prognosis and projected difficulties. The cancer was gone, with all teeth removed.

At the time of writing it is now eight years since I was told my maximum life expectancy was two years. I am well and there is no trace of the cancer at all. I know that this is only because God had worked in my life to stop the cancer from taking the natural course expected by the doctors. Isn't He wonderful?

Double Vision

My wife and I were attending a class on Monday evening at church. We had arrived fairly early and as the others started to file in, I looked round and saw two images of someone as he walked into the room. Initially I was worried but thought it may be just the bridge of my nose that caused my vision to be distorted. As the week progressed, the double vision was occurring again and again. I began feeling faint and unsteady on my feet.

I arranged to see the doctor on Friday. By then the double vision was becoming more regular. He was unsure as to the cause or the solution and arranged an appointment with an ear nose and throat (ENT) specialist. But that night, as I was driving home with my wife, the double vision started again: two cars coming towards me, two roads in front of me. I was very worried and we went straight to the hospital. The doctors examined me and then got second and third opinions. I was told that I had Bell's palsy as it was noticed that one side of my mouth was drooping. It was advised that I see a specialist and a daily dose of 30mg of steroids was prescribed.

On Sunday I went to church and by this stage I now had total double vision. It felt very awkward. I could not read the words of the hymns on the screen easily and everybody had an exact replica. A couple of friends prayed for me.

When I went to the hospital on Monday, the ENT specialist was baffled. He could see some symptoms of Bell's palsy but said he had never known it to affect anybody's eyesight. He said he wanted me to see an eye specialist so we queued for an hour before being seen by one. He looked at my eyes, then got a colleague to look and then said he wanted to refer me to another eye specialist. While waiting to see this latest practitioner, his assistant gave me an eye examination which showed that my left eye was viewing the same vision as my right eye but at a few centimetres difference. When the last eye specialist eventually examined my eyes he sent for three neurologists. They recommended a brain scan as soon as possible and rushed through an appointment for Thursday the following week. An increased dose of steroids was also prescribed which the hospital chemist was reluctant to dispense. The daily dose of steroids was now 500mg.

It feels lonely when you can't see. I was unable to work, drive, read or watch television. Walking outside was difficult. By Wednesday there was the odd spell of normal sight but it was rare. On Wednesday night my wife and I went to a small group meeting at church and they all prayed for me. I was hopeful it would go there and then but when I opened my eyes it was apparent that it was not to be the case. My double vision persisted. We drove home and went to bed. The next morning I woke up and blinked my eyes open. My vision was back to normal!

I still attended the hospital, as advised, for my brain scan the following week as I was worried about the cause of my impairment and did not want a reoccurrence of the condition. The results showed what was described to me as an 'Unidentified Brilliant Object', something that the medical team could not explain. I was told that my condition had completely cleared up and they were at a complete loss as to how to explain it. They suggested I should content myself with baffling the entire ENT, eye specialists and neurologists at the hospital!

ANDREW LAMIN

To the Faithful You Show Yourself Faithful
(Psalm 18:25)

A stalwart member of Huddersfield Christian Fellowship since joining in 1988, Andrew is regarded by many as its resident Bible expert. With his thorough command of the Bible, he is capable of mentally referencing limitless portions of scripture by chapter and verse, and has been called on to do so many times during services where the speaker has mislaid a section of text. This is not just head knowledge as the Word, and Andrew's comprehension of it, has seeped into his psychological make up, producing faith and tenacity of character as is demonstrated by his testimony.

'As a child I had my fair share of illnesses but the first signs of something more serious came during a games lesson when I was fifteen,' he begins. 'One minute I was vigorously pursuing members of another team around the school hall, the next, my arms and legs were not doing what I was telling them to and I crumpled into a heap on the floor. I was conscious of what was happening but unable to do anything about it, or for what seemed a long time, to pick myself up. In reality, I was back to normal before anyone arrived to see what was happening and, to avoid any embarrassing explanations, said that I had tripped and was now all right. The whole thing was very disconcerting, but I ignored it and hoped nothing like it would happen again. Unfortunately, it was the first of a great many episodes, reaching a point within a few months where I was getting ten or fifteen per hour. They were hardly ever serious, and I learned to live in such a way that they could be handled – avoiding sudden movement, or doing things that might leave me in embarrassing circumstances.'

Like many teenagers, Andrew had a great fear of seeming different or being singled out for special attention. 'I had seen how one boy who had epilepsy was treated,' he says. 'So I told nobody, and didn't go to a doctor until I left home in 1976. Being miles away from home, I finally felt able to go to a doctor who didn't know me or my family. He referred me to a specialist and told me not to drive – something that was not a problem for a student who couldn't afford such things anyway. After extensive tests, which proved very little, I was placed on medication, told that I was suffering from paroxysmal choreoathetosis, and again told not to drive. The medication made a huge difference, bringing me down to one or two attacks per hour. I got on with living, graduated in 1980 and came to live in West Yorkshire. I got a job in Cleckheaton and could get everywhere on foot or by bus and so I was able to cope quite easily.'

A few years later, however, his employer relocated to Manchester and Andrew found himself dependent on others to enable him to make the seventy-mile return trip to work as public transport proved a very lengthy process. 'This forced me to look hard at my medical condition,' he asserts. 'And as I had become a member of Huddersfield Christian Fellowship, a church that believes in prayer for healing, I went out to be prayed for at the first opportunity and stopped taking medication. After a very short time I was back where I had started with very frequent attacks. I quickly started taking the tablets again but I was not put off. I kept asking for prayer, and people kept praying for me. I would stop taking the tablets, the symptoms would become much more frequent and I would go back to taking the medication.

'Then in 1990 a prophet from Canada, who had never met me and knew nothing about me, came to our church and declared that God had shown him that I had an epileptic problem that He wanted to heal me of. This reinforced my determination and I kept on going out for prayer at every opportunity, though I had learned not to stop taking the tablets, believing that I would know when I had been healed. I was prayed for by all manner of people, even in Kenya on one occasion, but with no discernible results.'

In 1997, with the early retirement of his colleague who had faithfully driven him to work over the years, the pressure to do something about his condition increased. 'I went to my doctor who increased the dosage of the anti-convulsant from two to three a day,' he says. 'But I still had the same problems, greater side-effects and didn't consider that I was safe to drive.'

A year later, the Kenyan minister who had prayed for him in Nairobi and had become a good friend, visited Huddersfield and at the end of the evening meeting asked if anyone wanted prayer for healing. 'Nobody was surprised when I went out,' Andrew says drily, 'and he prayed much as others had done many times before. However, although nothing dramatic seemed to happen, I felt that something had changed and cut down the medication to one a day. Some months later I had experienced no further symptoms but my doctor had noticed that I was coming for repeat prescriptions at much longer intervals and asked to see me. I explained what had happened and remained on the much lower dose. After twelve months of no attacks, I applied for a driving licence and, at the age of forty-two, passed the test in February 2000. My licence was reviewed at intervals until 2005, when I was granted a licence to drive until my seventieth birthday, as I have remained entirely free from symptoms since that Sunday evening in 1998.'

Twenty-five years of convulsions, nine years of persevering in prayer and believing that he would be healed and Andrew's prayers were answered. Why his healing should have been of such a protracted nature is something that we cannot be privy to. However, we can be sure that 'suffering produces perseverance; perseverance, character; and character, hope. And hope does not disappoint us, because God has poured out his love into our hearts by the Holy Spirit, whom he has given us' (Romans 5:3-5). One thing is certain, Andrew understands the value of perseverance, and God has been faithful to honour that.

A Man Most Blessed

The first time I saw him in the early 1990s, Colin Cooper was preaching at the Sunday morning service in the spacious main hall of the former Huddersfield Christian Fellowship building in Northumberland Street. Dark-skinned, smartly-dressed, his crop of curly black hair kept short and neat, he was expounding on biblical principles and applying them to modern day life. Examples from the Old and New Testaments sprang to life as their relevance to a group of people in the twentieth century were revealed. His message was, and still is to this day, that the answers to all life's circumstances, mysteries and dilemmas can be found within the pages of this ancient, Holy Spirit-inspired tome. Although completed centuries ago, it is still 'as fresh as today's newspaper', as Colin likes to say. Indeed, Corrie Ten Boom, as she delved into this hidden treasure during her internment at the infamous Ravensbruck concentration camp during World War II, discovered in astonishment: 'Sometimes I would slip the Bible from its little sack with hands that shook, so mysterious had it become to me. It was new; it had just been written. I marvelled sometimes that the ink was dry. I had believed the Bible always, but reading it now had nothing to do with belief. It was simply a description of the way things were – of hell and heaven, of how men act and how God acts.'[7]

Warm-hearted, sunny and fun-loving, Colin is held in high esteem by his 700-strong (and still counting!) flock who see him living

---

7   Ten Boom, Corrie; with Sherrill, Elizabeth and Sherrill, John (2004 Edition) *The Hiding Place*, Hodder and Stoughton p 182

out the message he preaches. Far from being a remote figure pontificating from a platform, he actively gets involved in all aspects of his calling, from cleaning the church toilets to making himself available, together with his wife Sue, at any hour of the day or night for those in crisis. His congregation is his family and he cares for them as one who, on the Day of Judgement, will be required to provide a stricter account ('Not many of you should presume to be teachers, my brothers, because you know that we who teach will be judged more strictly' James 3:1) giving a reckoning not only for his own life but also for those over whom he has pastoral care.

Perhaps this paints a picture of a typical man of the cloth, one who can be found in hundreds of churches across the country, possibly coming from a religious background where faith is nurtured and encouraged. But Colin's early life was unconventional in the extreme and seemed to predestine him for a different type of future altogether …

'I was born in 1948 and was brought up in the 1950s and when I was a kid in my household there was never any love shown whatsoever,' he remembers. 'The only time that I ever remember my mother and father together was when they were fighting, and I remember, because I kinda liked both of them, I would say: "Come on Dad, come on Dad," "Come on Mum, come on Mum," and I didn't know which side to take. Never can I remember them ever putting their arms around me and saying: "We love you." I didn't know what that was. That was the kind of environment I was brought up in.'

Colin's young life was characterised by tragedy, starting with the one scenario a child conceivably fears most. 'I remember my father when he died. I remember the hurt of someone dying and passing out of the family.' Colin was not even ten at the time but this trauma was soon followed by another: his sister simply disappeared, never to be seen or heard of again. No reason was ever given to the young boy as to why, without warning, another family member had somehow passed into oblivion. 'I was young so they didn't bother explaining things to me,' he states. 'And then just after that, my brother was drowned,' he continues. 'He was three years older than me and he was drowned in the river up there in Newcastle and I remember the pain.' In a short space of time he had lost three close family members, leaving just himself and his mother to face the future alone together.

Events seemed to determine otherwise, though. One day, the shocked eleven-year-old watched in horror as his mother, wearing a glazed expression, advanced towards him, a huge kitchen knife in her hand. 'She came to me and she said, "I'm going to kill you",' Colin remembers. 'And I remember grabbing hold of her wrists in fear. I said: "Mum, whatever I've done, I'm sorry. Please, I'm sorry." She just looked and she said: "I'm going to kill you." Now, it was only just a minute or two but it seemed like an eternity, then she snapped to and wandered off.' A terrifying ordeal in anyone's book, but well before this time his mother's behaviour had been influenced by, and was the influence for, many unexplained and frightening happenings in the Cooper household.

'My mum used to be into all kinds of weird stuff,' he explains. 'She considered herself to be a witch. Things would go zipping across the wall, pictures would move by themselves, there would be strange noises and my mother would name the dead people walking through the room. I was taught how to conjure up the devil in the mirror. I even once saw the devil, his face glowing like a luminous mask, a short distance from our house and even though I had heard and seen many strange things as a young boy, that really unnerved me. My mother would put curses on people and they would actually work; she could also prophesy some things and I would see them come to pass. Because of all these things she was involved in, and the fact that my father, brother and sister were all gone, something must have snapped inside her because one day she came to me and she said: "Colin, I've been talking to your brother." Now, I didn't fully understand all these things and I said: "My brother? But he's dead, Mum." She said, "I know, but he was as real to me as you are standing here." Then she said: "I'm going to die," and within a month she was dead. You see, it was understood in the world my mother lived in, that once you saw a dead relative, your own death was imminent,' Colin explains. 'That's the power the devil has.'

He continues: 'In the Bible it says that whenever a person has died there is a gulf fixed and no-one can come back across that gulf. "And besides all this, between us and you a great chasm has been fixed, so that those who want to go from here to you cannot, nor can anyone cross over from there to us' (Luke 16:26)." Colin maintains that his mother's involvement in the occult meant that what she saw was actually something counterfeit from Hell and believes that people are deceived when they think they can contact someone from beyond the grave. 'I believe in a devil,' he says. 'And when I say a devil, I don't mean the guy with the bloodshot eyes and the horns and the tail and a pitchfork like the medieval pictures, but an evil being whose only plan and purpose is to get you because he hates you. If you are a Christian, he hates you, and if you're not a Christian he hates you, but the difference is, in God's family there is protection. Outside of God's family, you are open to the devil and his purposes and my mum was on the outside of God's family.'

At the time of his mother's death, Colin was not yet fifteen. 'I remember walking out into the garden and it was a starlit night, I remember this so clearly. And I thought: "If there was a God, why would these things happen to me? My father's dead, my sister's gone, my brother's dead, my mother's dead – my whole family. If there was a God, He wouldn't allow this to happen to me". Have you noticed that everybody blames God for the bad things?' he digresses. 'There's just something in us that does it. You very rarely get anybody saying, "Well isn't the Lord good?" unless they really know Jesus, but they blame God for the bad things.'

Colin was taken into care and housed with 'a very bad-tempered woman with some terrible attitudes'. The embittered young man, who as a young boy had been pressurised by his mother into physically attacking anyone who verbally abused him because of his skin colour 'she often used a dog lead with a chain on the end, she would whip me with it on the back and legs. I would have weals coming up with blood spurting out' now formed a local gang with some friends. 'Fights were the norm,' he says. 'We would meet on a bridge over the River Tyne at Newburn to face another gang from the town on the other side of the river. The clash would be in the centre of the bridge. I was always in the centre front of the group, urging them on. Bicycle chains, bottles, planks of wood, bricks, knives and even the odd sword would appear. How I did not get severely injured is a mystery, other than I could move very fast. Some guys would get badly injured, but keeping to a code of not "squealing", they always professed to have had an accident.'

Earning the nickname 'Cass', after the boxing champion, Cassius Clay (later named Muhammed Ali), he found himself in jail on an indictment of grievous bodily harm for smashing and grinding a beer glass into his opponent's skull. 'This is when something began to change in my life,' he recollects. 'I was lying down in the jail and I was looking around those four white walls … and the beds, they weren't luxury like today. They were just like logs split down the middle and turned with the rounded bit on the bottom and the flat bit on the top. And the pillow was the same! I tell you, I believe they should be like that today and then guys wouldn't be in a hurry to get back there. I was lying down and I thought: "This is a crazy way to live. When I get out of here, I'm going to turn over a new leaf and I'm going to fit into society. I'm going to get a job and live a better life." And I meant it.'

On his release, however, his gang friends, who had always insisted that 'unless you've been in jail, you ain't no man', were waiting for him outside and Colin, who felt he had earned this accolade and was proud of his 'Cool Cass' image, fell in with them once more. Looking back he says: 'You'll never see a leopard change his spots. It's impossible, and for a real changed life, you need something greater than a determination to change. I could not change because I had a certain nature and lifestyle and a certain mould that programmed me to live like that.'

Sent back to live with his former carer, he was soon given his marching orders for returning home late from a night out. 'She hit me with a broom and told me to leave the house immediately,' he says. By this time he was seventeen and earning money as a farmhand and coal deliverer. After finishing his day's work, he would be dropped off and head straight for the coal storage shed for the night. This makeshift shelter was to become his home. Unsurprisingly, the cold, damp British weather and lack of even the most basic of amenities soon told on his health. 'I remember just lying on the coals and I had the shivers because of my lifestyle. I was shaking and I remember thinking: "Man, I can't go on like this."

'Then suddenly,' Colin pauses. 'The clock began to tick. God began to set it in motion. Now, I'd never been to church in my life. I'd never said a prayer in my life, in fact I didn't know what a prayer *was*! So I said a prayer! Can you believe that? Now, if I'd said that prayer in a normal church today, the way I said it then, I would probably have been thrown out. It went something like this: "Hey God! If you're real, you get me an apartment and I'll believe in you." Man, was that pure blackmail or was that blackmail? But you see, God doesn't look on the refined prayers of a person, He looks on the heart and He says: "I know what the heart is saying and I set that thing in motion." And the very next day, I was in an apartment!'

Coincidence? Not in Colin's book. He had been trying to rent an apartment for two years. 'And if you could have seen me back then, you'd have understood why I couldn't get one. Because in the 1960s, especially in the North East where I lived, man if you were mixed race that was tough enough, but mixed race and a weirdo, man that was doubly tough!' Dressed in a knee-length purple velvet jacket complete with long chiffon scarf, black velvet trousers and crocodile shoes, his hair 'like an explosion in a mattress factory' and sporting earrings (unusual for a man in those days) he would turn up for viewing appointments. 'And I just remember every time I knocked on the door, the landlady would come with a smile. Then she would see me:
"Are you Cooper?"

"Yes"

"Oh, I'm sorry, it's gone."

Slam! The door was shut in my face.'

On this occasion, however, the day after his first ever prayer and specific request, he simply knocked on the door of an advertised apartment and was immediately granted tenancy. Unable to believe his good fortune, Colin thanked his new landlady, adding that it was the first time he had received a positive response. 'That's probably because you're black,' was the prompt reply. The apartment was small and sparsely furnished. A bed, bureau and rug made up its contents and fresh air was provided twenty-four hours a day courtesy of a bullet hole in the window. But to Colin it was paradise.

It was also directly opposite the biggest church in the city! One day an open air service was held and Colin and a group of his friends walked over 'to have a laugh at these people standing in a circle and shouting'. He was approached by someone from the church group not much older than himself who asked him a direct question. 'If you died tonight, where would you spend eternity?' Taken aback by his straight talking and intrigued that, according to his questioner it was possible to know one's destination after death, Colin agreed to meet him the following week to attend a church service.

That Sunday, setting foot inside a church for the first time in his life and taking in his surroundings, not so much absorbing the atmosphere and interior of this place of worship, as 'checking the girls out', the service passed him by altogether. As the proceedings drew to a close, however, and Colin prepared to leave, his young Christian friend again broached the subject of eternity. 'He explained the Gospel very clearly,' says Colin. 'Although I had not heard a word the preacher had said, I was now beginning to understand a little.' On the strength of that explanation, he asked the God he did not yet know to forgive him for all his past wrongdoings and handed over his life to the One who had purchased his redemption and eternal life at so great a cost to Himself. 'And nothing instantly happened in the church,' he remarks. 'But as I was walking down the street something came over me and this joy just began to overwhelm me as I began to understand that Jesus had given me a new life. The street was packed with people and (remember "Cool Cass") I just leapt in the middle of the street. Something of the joy of God, of the joy of Jesus, had come into my life.'

The move to the little apartment opposite the church had proved, literally, to be a Godsend, providing Colin not only with a new home but a new life. Moreover, he had made a very good friend in one of his co-tenants. A student at Newcastle University, this young man's parents lived in Canada and so he, like Colin, was to all intents and purposes alone. 'We became great buddies,' explains Colin. 'We used to share our clothes and cook our meals together and he started to put some kind of culture into me. He would take me to art galleries and I used to take him to discos and we kind of swapped ideas.'

One thing they didn't share, however, was his new friend's proclivity for drugs. 'He took all kinds of stuff. He kept his hashish in a vase with daffodils and he stole chloroform from the university to sniff and get high on. He would come into my room:
"Hey, Cass."

"What?"

"Switch on, man.""Of course now I was a Christian and I'd say: "Well, I don't do those things any more, I'm a Christian." Then I would give him a little leaflet explaining about church and stuff. I never told him about Jesus but I invited him to church and he would look at me and you could see the despair in his eyes. "Oh man, you're cuckoo," he would say.'

One day though, his young friend seemed deeply troubled. 'I feel that this world is like a big rock and I'm the only person on it, drifting in a black void and I want to get off,' he explained. He said he needed to talk but Colin was just on his way out to a party and told him that they would do so on his return. 'And I remember him turning his back and walking out of the room,' Colin says.

Returning home that night, the first sight that met his eyes was the police outside his building. After establishing Colin's identity, one of the officers told him something for which he was completely unprepared: his friend had drunk a bottle of chloroform and died. 'And I remember again being faced with death but in a different setting,' says Colin. 'I walked into my room and I remember just falling to my knees, and it wasn't holiness or anything, I was just so wiped out! Now, I'd never cried since I was a kid because of my lifestyle, but that night I began to cry and I remember just weeping and weeping and the tears rolling down. It wasn't just because I'd lost this guy who was like a brother to me, although that was one of the reasons. The other was I had never told him about Jesus. I'd invited him to church, I'd given him a little leaflet with a message on it about Jesus but I had never *told him about Jesus* and I knew that if I had told him about the change that Jesus could make in his life, he would be alive right at that moment. I cried and said:

"God, forgive me, forgive me. I didn't tell him about Jesus.'" His friend's shocking and untimely death had brought home to him the transitory nature of life and he would never again shirk from speaking about the One who had the power to transform lives and save humanity from an eternity in torment.

Life went on and Colin started work in a department store on the chicken counter. At about this time he met Sue, a minister's daughter, at a party. 'She was from another church,' he says. 'The first time I noticed her was when she leaned back on her chair and broke the glass in a cabinet,' he remembers fondly. 'She was extremely embarrassed, but the noise of the glass breaking drew my attention and I thought she was cute, breaking the glass and all that. Then I noticed she had very nice legs.' Colin asked to walk her home and was disappointed to learn that she had already accepted a lift from a friend. Before her departure, however, Sue had found out a little bit about him from mutual friends and soon afterwards 'accidentally' bumped into him at the store. 'I tell people she came in because she found me irresistible,' is Colin's take on the story. They saw each other every day after that and Colin recalls meeting her family of high-flyers for the first time. Her brothers, one an accountant, one a surveyor and the other an insurance broker, and her brother-in-law, a physicist, asked him about his job. 'I sell chickens,' was Colin's prompt and honest retort.

Perhaps in Sue's family's eyes he wasn't seen as an achiever and therefore not the best candidate as a prospective husband, but the two were in love and soon married. Not long after this, Colin started to believe that God had something better lined up for him: 'I was looking through the jobs in the newspaper and my eye fell on this one job. I said: "Hey, Sue! Have you seen this job?"' Sue peered over his shoulder at the advertisement, then back at her husband. Always supportive, she tried to break it to him gently. 'I believe God wants to bless you and has got better things for you,' she started. 'But that salary is double what you're getting now and for the salary alone there will be a lot of people lining up for it and they will all have degrees in science like it's asking for. You haven't got one!' Undeterred by his wife's logic, Colin posted off his application and waited. Contrary to Sue's expectations, very soon afterwards he was asked to attend an interview.

On the due date he turned up for his appointment. His interviewer glanced at the curriculum vitae in front of him and kicked off the proceedings:

'Mr Cooper?'

'Yes.'

'Have you got a degree in science?'

'No.'

'Well, have you got any A-levels?'

'No.'

'Well, what about O-levels?'

'No.'

'Well what have you got?'

'I haven't got anything.'

Not an auspicious start. Colin then proceeded to tell him about himself. His questioner listened attentively before pronouncing his telling verdict. Colin returned home. 'They're going to let me know,' he told Sue. 'I told you so,' she sighed.

That afternoon the telephone rang. 'Oh, good afternoon,' said the male voice on the other end, giving his name. 'I just wanted to tell you, Mr Cooper, that the job's yours and when can you start?' When a beaming Colin replaced the receiver, he just had one thing to say to his astounded wife: 'I TOLD YOU SO!!'

The job, as a medical representative, entailed a move to Derby (two hundred and sixty miles south of Newcastle, where they lived). There the young couple joined a local church where Colin was soon asked to join the team as a youth leader. He accepted the position and found to his surprise that he could preach. Within a year his young charges had grown from a handful to a hundred and Colin began to see that God perhaps had a different future in store for him.

One evening he was thinking about ongoing business deals as he drove to his hotel after another day on the road when he heard a voice distinctly saying: 'You are wasting your time on temporal things.' 'It was not like some person speaking or a gut feeling, yet it was clear,' Colin recollects. 'It's only now I realise that it was one of the few occasions when the Holy Spirit spoke clearly and audibly to me.' Arriving back at his room a little shaken, he phoned Sue as was his daily practice when he was working away from home. Determined not to tell her about the experience 'because she might think I had flipped,' he talked about his day. But Sue's perceptiveness was finely honed. There was something Colin wasn't telling her, she just knew it. 'What's wrong?' she asked time and again as the conversation continued and Colin persistently denied that anything was amiss. Eventually, however, he reluctantly related his experience in the car, expecting perhaps some gentle ridicule. Instead there was just a silence. Sue later told him that she knew God was calling them to the ministry, but was anxious about the prospect as, being a minister's daughter, she knew only too well the pressures involved in this type of vocation.

Notwithstanding, the couple started working full-time for Home Missions, an arm of the Assemblies of God Church which planted churches in areas where they were most needed. Throwing themselves heart and soul into their first venture, they sold their home and moved into a two-roomed cellar, investing the proceeds into the new church they were building with the money helping to pay for a minibus, furniture, books and other assorted overheads. By this time it was the late 1970s and they had two small children in tow. Their accommodation left a lot to be desired. Human waste would run down the walls as the overhead sewer periodically overflowed (Colin could regularly be found up to his arms in excrement as he struggled to unblock the drains); the cold and damp encouraged visits from slugs which left long silver trails on the blankets of the camp-beds they put down each night and mice nibbled daily on their food. At the time, Colin remembers thinking: 'Is this ministry? What have I done?' With hindsight, he now understands that the hard times were instrumental in building up their characters for the work, not yet revealed, that lay ahead of them. 'The church soon grew,' says Colin. 'And we learned a lot.'

Colin moved on to pastor other churches and in 1987 was asked to lead a small group of people in Huddersfield, a mill town in the north of England. The family unit though, was happy and settled in southern England. Moreover the children were now teenagers and due to take their final high school exams. Both Colin and Sue, however, felt that God was calling them to make this move and therefore they had no option but to obey.

Under Colin's leadership, Huddersfield Christian Fellowship began to steadily increase in numbers. In time the premises were extended to include offices, youth rooms, a coffee and book shop as well as a main meeting hall, seating 400, where the services were held. When the congregation had grown to such an extent that church services had to be video-relayed to an overspill area in another part of the building, new premises were sought and in 1999, Huddersfield Christian Fellowship moved to its newly-renovated, purpose-built sanctuary, Harvest House. A former factory with a seating capacity of 800 and furnished in restful purples and greens, Harvest House was intended to be the Fellowship's home for many years to come. Within the space of six years, however, the building was packed to overflowing, prompting the church leadership team to hold two Sunday morning services to accommodate the enlarged congregation and to look for a new and bigger site. In the meantime Colin, who had been forging links with other churches, was approached by Pastor Dick Iverson, the founder of Ministers' Fellowship International, to be responsible for the establishment of a European expression of this ecclesiastical support network. Huddersfield Christian Fellowship gave its enthusiastic approval to the proposal and in 2001, under Colin's direction, Ministers' Fellowship Europe came into being.

To put this into context, many years before when Huddersfield Christian Fellowship was still in its infancy, Colin had received a prophetic word during a Sunday morning service that he would be leading a team in Europe. At the time it seemed unimaginable, but now the prophecy has truly been fulfilled. Today, Huddersfield Christian Fellowship has influence and supports churches not only in Europe, but also in the USA, South America, Canada, India and various African nations, to say nothing of those in the United Kingdom.

Reflecting back on his life, Colin feels that he is a 'man most blessed'. 'From a non-start in life I met Jesus and He took a foolish vessel and confounded the mighty.

Brothers, think of what you were when you were called. Not many of you were wise by human standards; not many were influential; not many were of noble birth.
But God chose the foolish things of the world to shame the wise; God chose the weak things of the world to shame the strong.
He chose the lowly things of this world and the despised things and the things that are not – to nullify the things that are,
so that no-one may boast before him.
(1 Corinthians 1:26-29)

All Jesus needs is a willing person to work through,' he asserts.

And Colin should know; his life is the proof.

by Colin Cooper

Perhaps you have read the whole book, or just some of the testimonies, and have arrived at this page. Perhaps you, in common with the people you have just met between these pages, are facing a crisis or find yourself in an unbearable situation with nowhere to turn. Perhaps you think that you have made so many big mistakes that you feel God couldn't possibly love you or forgive you. Or, perhaps like me as a teenager, you need to know where you will go when you die. If so, then this book is for you.

Jesus loves you, yes YOU. He will forgive you and help you in your personal situation, whatever the circumstances. He longs to have a relationship with you. But, as you may have heard before, He is a gentleman. He knocks at your door and waits for an invitation to come in. You see, the door only has one handle, and it's on your side. It's up to you! Do you want to have the assurance that Jesus is beside you every step of the way as you walk through life? He may not take all your problems away but He promises to guide you through them if you allow Him to.

The people in this book, and all those who have asked Jesus into their lives, will testify that it's the best decision they have ever made. It could just be that God ordained this day, this time, for you, so that you can make that life-changing decision for yourself. Don't miss out on His blessings! Even if you have always known that God existed and you perhaps attended, or attend a Christian church, but can never specifically remember a time when you invited Jesus into your life, make that time now.

Would you like to take that step? Let's take it together. Just say these words and mean them.

Lord Jesus, thank you for loving me. Thank you for dying on the Cross for me and taking the punishment for all my sins. I'm sorry when I've done things wrong in the past, but with your help, I know I can live a better life. Jesus, I ask You into my life and acknowledge You as my Lord and Saviour.

Thank you Jesus.

Amen.

References

1. Pearsall J (Ed) (2002) *Concise Oxford English Dictionary* 10th Edition Revised, Oxford University Press

2. Wilkerson, David; with Sherrill, Elizabeth and Sherrill, John (2002 Edition) *The Cross and the Switchblade*, Zondervan p 84

3. Pearsall J (Ed) (2002) *Concise Oxford English Dictionary* 10th Edition Revised, Oxford University Press

4. Pullinger, Jackie with Quicke, Andrew (2006) *Chasing the Dragon*, Hodder and Stoughton

5. Mitson, Eileen; Goss, Steve (2005) *Songs of Freedom Stories of Lives Transformed by the Deep Power of Christ*, Monarch Books p 153

6. Mitson, Eileen; Goss, Steve (2005) *Songs of Freedom Stories of Lives Transformed by the Deep Power of Christ*, Monarch Books p 153

7. Ten Boom, Corrie; with Sherrill, Elizabeth and Sherrill, John (2004 Edition) *The Hiding Place*, Hodder and Stoughton p 182

About the Author

Basia Armitage was born to Polish parents in 1960 and was brought up with her sister and brother in Leeds. She lives with her husband, Peter, in Huddersfield and has three step-daughters.

Printed in the United Kingdom by
Lightning Source UK Ltd., Milton Keynes
137348UK00001B/97-507/P